Positively Toward the Negative

Surviving the Trump-Led Attack
on American Values
and Basic Human Decency

John Sheirer

ISBN: 9798683531928

Photos on the cover and on page 155 by the author.

Photo of the author on page 161 by Betsy Sheirer.

https://scanticbooks.blogspot.com
Facebook: Scantic Books

Dedication

For Emily and Matthew.
When we're long gone,
the world will be theirs.
Let's leave them a better world.

Positively Toward the Negative

I'm still here.
I'm still here.

And I tested
very positively
in another sense.

So, this morning.
Yeah.

I tested positively
toward negative.

Right?
So, no.

I tested perfectly
this morning.
Meaning I tested
negative.

But that's a way
of saying it:

Positively
toward the
negative.

- Donald Trump -
Unintentionally summing up his terrible presidency
in terrible poetry
after his COVID-19 test, May 21, 2020.

Table of Contents

A Note on the Order

Except for the introductory section of this book, these columns appear in chronological order beginning based on their original monthly publication in the *Daily Hampshire Gazette*. The first one dates back to May 2016, the first column after my previous collection of columns, *Make Common Sense Common Again*. Please feel free to read these pieces in chronological order, reverse order, or even at random. Think of this book as a time machine that can deposit the reader in any month during the past four years. In a world dominated by 24-hour news cycles and social media clickbait headlines that change by the minute, we can all benefit from savoring each snapshot in time and experiencing important issues with a fuller consideration of the context than can be gained by skimming a status update or a tweet.

- Introduction -

Positively Toward the Negative

September 2020

Writing a monthly column illustrates the elastic nature of time. So much happens in the preceding month that it's impossible to cover it all within the word-count limit. So you identify a trend or event and explore its significance. But you can't dig too deeply because a Monday column has to be submitted on the previous Thursday to allow for editorial review and production.

For example, my column last month fact-checked the silly notion that Joe Biden is cognitively impaired. Between submitting the column on Thursday and publication on Monday, we saw Biden vigorously ride a bike while making a quick-witted, perfectly lucid joke. Then Biden looked great at his convention. Donald Trump, conversely, painfully mispronounced "Yosemite," lied and misused the presidency as a prop throughout his convention, and seemed profoundly confused in softball interviews.

The people still claiming that Biden is incompetent sound even more ridiculous than before. My column was retroactively obsolete.

A monthly column can shed light on particular moments, and the accumulation of these moments illuminates a longer time period. My 2016 book, *Make Common Sense Common Again: Exploring Current Events in the Age of Mass Confusion,* was primarily composed of my *Gazette* columns from the previous four years and explored the context that led to Trump's election. I certainly didn't predict that result, but the book helped me (and, I hope, readers) understand how something so unexpectedly terrible could happen.

This new book, *Positively Toward the Negative: Surviving the Trump-led Attack on American Values and Basic Human Decency,* collects my columns since 2016 and examines our nation's struggle with Trumpism. What can those years tell us about the upcoming election and beyond?

The biggest takeaway from the last four years is that Trump has been a failed president who clearly doesn't deserve reelection. He has lied constantly, stolen credit for Obama's economy, become a hero to white supremacists, surrounded himself with criminals and incompetents, botched responses to natural disasters, mistreated refugees, violated norms and traditions, committed impeachable crimes, attacked peaceful protestors, used religion as a prop, disparaged our military and intelligence agencies, insulted our citizens and allies, squandered American goodwill worldwide, coddled dictators, demonized our free press, enabled polluters, sabotaged our Post Office, coopted our justice system, illegally used our White House for his political convention, lethally mismanaged a pandemic, put our social security at risk, and even undermined our electoral process.

Trump hasn't been horrible in a vacuum. He wafts on a flood of right-wing misinformation and clings to lifelines from Republican enablers in Congress who daily trade their integrity for Trump slashing wealthy and corporate taxes and appointing extremist judges. Republican policies were damaging for the country long before Trump. But regressive Republicanism blended with chaotic Trumpism has brewed a toxic maelstrom that threatens to drown what Lincoln called the "better angels" of our nation's nature.

Democrats haven't been perfect during the past four years, but they've kept the country afloat and herald a far better future. Joe Biden and Kamala Harris weren't everyone's first choice, but they represent an opportunity to return dignity, honesty, integrity, intelligence, common sense, and core American values to the White House. They'll surround themselves with outstanding professionals instead of sycophants and opportunists. They're farther left than progressives think but nowhere near the radical Communists portrayed by Republicans. They're certainly not anti-God, as the unholy Trump would have you believe.

Biden won't turn America into a hellscape of riots and crime, as Trump claims. The Trump-supporting vigilantes who have disrupted peaceful protests thrive under Trump's "good people" coded language. Trump's divisive rhetoric and the draconian policing policies he supports have instigated much of the violence that Biden and Harris have condemned.

If Democrats also hold the House and retake the Senate, we have a chance for legislation to improve the lives of the vast majority of Americans. Think of the progress that can be made in battling the pandemic, reinvigorating the middle-class, making the tax system fairer, providing access to health care, healing the environment, promoting voting rights, reforming criminal justice, enacting effective and humane immigration policy, and championing common-sense gun-safety laws. That's how progress works: steadily forward, positively toward the positive.

If we win, our national recovery won't be immediate or even swift. I hope to spend the next four years writing about good ideas and legislation and policies, about leaders who represent all Americans, not just a privileged few, about how this country shook off authoritarianism and division and hate and moved forward, slowly, bumpily, steadily, overcoming ugly pockets of regression and the last gasps of Trumpism—toward our more perfect union.

Trump has left the nation damaged and reeling. We can't be apathetic or deluded. We should all see now just how devastating for America another Trump term would be. He won't redeem himself in the time it takes this column to go to print or in the month before my next column.

These last four years have been capped off by 2020, a year that future historians will render as one of the worst in our nation's history, a year marinated in suffering, violence, and preventable death. But if good people vote in large numbers, we have the opportunity to make sure 2020 doesn't end with a plunge backward to 2016.

Restroom Ridiculousness

May 2016

The restroom at my workplace is just twenty paces from my office, a proximity that has saved my dignity countless times. I'm incapable of the math that would reveal the hours I've spent in that room during the past twenty-three years. Let's just say that I've done a lot of reading.

In all those years, I've never once questioned the gender identity of the person in the next stall. That's none of my business as I go about my own private business. So the recent spate of anti-LGBT "bathroom bills" being pushed by Republican legislatures in various states makes me cringe.

One book that I read at least parts of during my workplace bathroom visits is Jenny Boylan's memoir, *She's Not There*. The book originally caught my eye because of how much I had in common with the author. We were both born in rural Pennsylvania and went on to become writers and college professors in New England. I enjoy reading memoirs that connect with my own experiences.

But Boylan's book also drew my attention because of a major difference in our lives. She grew up with the constant knowledge that she was actually a woman, rather than the man her body presented to the world. I've always known that my body matched my identity, so I had to step far outside my experience to relate to Boylan's life story.

Many other memoirs have taken me beyond my own limited life. I've never been pregnant, but Elizabeth McCracken's *An Exact Replica of a Figment of My Imagination* let me share the heartbreak of her miscarriage. I didn't move from Iran to the United States as a child in the 1970s, but Firoozeh Dumas's *Funny in Farsi* showed me the humor and humanity of her life as the ultimate outsider during turbulent times. I've never had a facial disfigurement, but Lucy Grealy's *Autobiography of a Face* let me see the world staring back at her. I'm not an autistic math genius, but David Tammet's *Born on a Blue Day* fascinated me with his perception of the world. I don't have Alzheimer's, but Thomas DeBaggio's *Losing My Mind* immersed me into the physical and mental disorientation that accompanied his deterioration.

Reading about the lives of people different from ourselves helps us develop empathy. No one would toss a book in the trash and claim that that pregnancy is a myth, that Autism, Alzheimer's, or facial disfigurement don't exist, that nobody's life is affected by his or her country of origin. That would violate basic human empathy and common sense. Life is so much more than what passes through our individual eyeballs into the blob of electrified gelatin housed beneath our Red Sox caps.

Yet many people claim that identifying as one gender while being born in the body of another is somehow imaginary. Doesn't that view show a shocking lack of empathy and common sense as well? What is it about the notion of being trans that inspires some Republicans to make laws discriminating against where people use the bathroom, something that the vast majority of Americans take for granted?

Another book I've read in my workplace restroom is Tarō Gomi's classic, *Everyone Poops*. I enjoy sharing that one with students in my Children's Literature classes to show that kid's books cover a wide range of human behaviors. The lesson is that we all use the restroom even if it's a subject we don't dwell on in polite society. So why do some conservatives want to regulate such a universal and personal act based on discrimination against gender identity?

Republicans making these discriminatory laws claim they're just trying to keep children safe in public restrooms. All of us empathize with keeping children safe. But there's no evidence that trans people are a danger to children or that sex offenders dress up as another gender to commit their crimes in restrooms. Statistically, children are far more likely to be molested by a close male family member or a trusted authority figure than by a trans person. A prime example is Dennis Hastert, the former Republican Speaker of the House, recently sentenced to jail time for being a serial child molester while he was a high school teacher and coach decades ago. That criminal certainly didn't wear a dress.

What about empathy for the actual threats that trans people face in public restrooms? Studies show that roughly two-thirds of trans people have been harassed over restroom use. This isn't an abstract political issue. Real human beings are being threatened. My friend Linda takes precautions every time her trans wife Grace uses a public restroom. "I want people to have empathy for my beautiful wife," Linda said. "Barring empathy, I want her to be left alone. She's not hurting anyone—she's just being who she is."

Linda continued, "I want the law to protect my wife, not put her at risk. That's why we have laws, isn't it?" Yes, it is. We all just want to feel safe while using the restroom that best fits who we are. Is it really so difficult to accept that our fellow human beings all just want empathy, safety, and a sense of belonging?

Evidence is a Virtue

June 2016

While waiting for a staff meeting to begin a few weeks ago, a colleague sat next to me, leaned in, and whispered conspiratorially, "So, which pile of crap are you voting for in November?"

He smiled as if sharing a favorite joke that he'd recited before but found pleasing enough to retell. He calls himself "moderate" but hardly ever discusses politics.

"I don't plan to vote for any pile of crap," I replied, wishing that the meeting had started on time. "I plan to vote for a very strong candidate with a long record of public service and great views on the issues."

"Come on," my colleague replied. "We both know that Clinton and Trump are exactly the same."

"Really?" I asked. "Have you actually looked at their proposals, listened to them, or researched their histories? They're pretty much exact opposites."

"No—just a feeling I have," he said, surprised by my insistence.

"What about evidence to back up those feelings?" I asked.

"They're exactly the bleeping same," he answered (only he didn't say "bleeping"). "I don't need evidence."

Throughout the meeting, I had trouble getting his last comment out of my mind: "I don't need evidence." That staff meeting focused on evidence regarding recent policy changes. Why does my colleague care about evidence at work but not for his political views?

His comments were on my mind when I got home and signed onto Facebook. Amid the usual cat videos and bacon-based recipes, a friend from high school shared a scathing report about ALEC, the right-wing, corporate-funded group that feeds terrible legislation to Republicans in Congress and state governments. His post surprised me, considering that he's a lifelong Republican.

I commented that I was glad he'd posted the report because it showed how the Republican Party had been serving special interest groups rather than their constituents. My friend replied that he wasn't agreeing with any of my "liberal spin." He claimed that the report showed that everyone in government was corrupt, not just Republicans.

I replied with links to evidence that showed ALEC is a conservative group that works with about 98% Republican politicians. "If you have any evidence that Democrats are influenced by groups like this, I'd be happy to see it," I added.

He responded, "I'm not interested in evidence. I know that Democrats are just as bleeping bad" (again, not really "bleeping").

How can someone have a discussion about politics without even being interested in evidence?

Most of the people I know who form their views without evidence are conservatives or right-leaning, self-described "moderates." The worst of them love to hammer President Obama as a foreign Socialist who hates America and only got elected because of voter fraud. These folks tend to be Trump supporters who believe that their candidate has a secret plan to defeat terrorism and will lead an economic resurgence because he is a magnificent business professional and the ultimate classy guy. Obviously, whole mountain ranges of evidence (and basic common sense) dispute their claims.

Liberals, in my experience, are generally fact-based folks. The vast majority of Bernie Sanders and Hillary Clinton supporters, for example, support their views with evidence. Unfortunately, the irrational "Bernie-or-Bust" folks are an exception. I recently found myself in a Facebook discussion with a liberal Hillary-hater who ranted that Clinton, "isn't a liberal and has never been a liberal."

"The evidence doesn't support that view," I countered, referencing several websites that cataloged Clinton's voting record and statements on various issues showing that she has been a liberal throughout her career.

The Bernie-or-Buster replied, "She doesn't really believe in liberal causes, no matter what she says or how she voted."

"So you reject Clinton's words and votes as evidence of her views?" I asked. "Does it take mind-reading to satisfy your standards?"

"The bleeping evidence is self-evident," she replied. "Nothing will change my mind."

She didn't say "bleeping" either, of course. No one ever says "bleeping" when arguing without evidence. I left the conversation with a snarky remark along the lines of, "Please tell us when you find Hillary's Kenyan birth certificate."

Her reply reminded me uncomfortably of the debate between creationist Ken Ham and Bill Nye, "The Science Guy." When asked what would change their views, Ham's response could be summed up as, "nothing." Nye's reply focused on one word: "evidence."

"The evidence is self-evident," sounds more like snake handlers than reasonable liberals discussing politics. Sanders himself whiffed badly when asked at the New York debate for evidence that Clinton was doing favors for Wall Street. Even he couldn't support claims that Clinton is some sort of closet Republican.

President Obama recently said, "Ignorance is not a virtue." He was clearly talking about Trump, but his words reach farther than the man who currently exemplifies thumbing his nose at evidence and embracing ignorance.

As Thomas Paine noted in his writings that helped spur the American Revolution, when we argue with someone who doesn't respect reason, we are "administering medicine to the dead." A sad corollary to Paine's observation is that some people today have abandoned evidence as the basic building block of reason. Whether someone is moderate, conservative, or liberal, the rejection of evidence is terrible citizenship.

Trump Faces Veep Dilemma

July 2016

The worst job I ever had was back in high school—using a pitchfork to clean the livestock stalls after the country fair ended. But that task was downright delightful compared with the manure slinging involved in being Donald Trump's running mate.

As pundits speculate about who will take on this impossible task, let's explore a list of suspects (assuming Trump hasn't already cursed an unfortunate soul with his choice by the time this column is published).

Primary competitors usually make a muddy puddle of potential running mates, and this election cycle is murkier than most. A whopping sixteen other candidates sought the Republican nomination, so we would think there might be plenty to choose from.

Ted Cruz finished second, but he has called Trump a "pathological liar," a "narcissist," and a "rat," among other colorful criticisms. Well, that might be awkward on the campaign trail.

Marco Rubio won a few states and was a Republican establishment favorite, but he implied that Trump has a small ... umm ... you know what. There's not enough mind bleach in the world to scrub that thought away. Thanks for nothing, Marco.

John Kasich said that Trump would lead the nation on a "path to darkness" that is "the antithesis of all that American has meant for the last 240 years." "Path to Darkness 2016!" is a more apt bumper sticker than Trump's deplorable slogan, "Make America Great Again!"

After endorsing Trump, Ben Carson became perhaps the worst campaign surrogate ever, flattering Trump with such commendations as, "He has some major defects—there's no question about it," and "Are there better people [for president]? Probably." Hillary Clinton's campaign could make an excellent ad out of Carson's "endorsement" of Trump.

Trump's most likely running mate among his former opponents is Chris Christie, who is leading Trump's ridiculously premature "transition team." But the notoriously hot-headed New Jersey governor once said of Trump, "I just don't think that he's suited to be president of the United States." Christie will most likely be transitioning back to the bridges of New Jersey.

Another Trump endorser is Jimmy McMillan, the founder of "The Rent is too Damn High Party." Yes, that's real. But considering McMillan is African-American and Trump has been sued for not renting to African-Americans, that match doesn't seem too damn likely.

Perhaps Trump could select one of the high-ranking Republicans in Congress who have whole-heartedly endorsed him. (Please insert cricket chirps here.)

One of the few Republicans who has campaigned enthusiastically (and incoherently) for Trump is Sarah Palin. She already has experience as a losing VP candidate, so she'll be best prepared for the drubbing Hillary will give the Donald in November. Another former party luminary rumored for VP is Newt Gingrich, whose main qualifications seem to be that he rivals Trump in scandals, con artistry, and ex-wives.

Trump could "honor" our Bay State and select former short-term Senator Scott Brown, himself once considered a presidential possibility. Trump has even been imitating Brown's racist criticism of Elizabeth Warren's Native American ancestry. That worked out so well for Brown that he now spends his time pimping weight-loss pills instead of his former job serving his Wall Street overlords in Congress.

Trump has gotten so much free corporate media coverage that he could consider what passes for "professional journalists" these days. MSNBC's Joe Scarborough, who once salivated over the multiple Trump appearances on the allegedly liberal network, recently started a tepid Twitter war with the wannabe "Commander in Tweet," so he's probably out of the running.

Fox News's Sean Hannity has been Trump's biggest cheerleader at the propaganda wing of the Republican Party. He has a history as an apologist for criminals such as George Zimmerman and Cliven Bundy, which could translate well in defending Trump. "Fox and Friends" gave Trump a forum for his "Birther" nonsense four years ago, so any of those interchangeable morning hosts would be comfortable helping to build Trump's wall.

Trump's negative ratings are so high that he could consider someone even less popular. One possibility is Martin "Pharma Bro" Shkreli, the smirk-faced, disgraced drug industry CEO. Shkreli has praised Trump and clearly sees him as a role model when gouging patients for unspeakable profits on AIDS medication. It's only a matter of time before Maury Povich says of Trump's relationship with Shkreli, "You are the father!"

If all else fails, Trump could choose a fellow reality TV star. Those "Real Housewives" all seem to be Republicans and as fake-wealthy as Trump. As an added bonus, Trump might find his fourth wife from among the youngest in the group.

Sensible people would rather clear manure with their bare hands than ponder being Trump's Vice President. Being so closely aligned with Trump would require an extremely high tolerance for repeated embarrassment along with correspondingly low standards for honesty, knowledge of the issues, and basic human decency.

Hmm ... maybe that's the answer. The most appropriate candidate to be Trump's running mate is ... Trump himself! His ego is certainly "yuuuuge" enough to hold both positions simultaneously. And he'd probably be happy to take on the second job if he could find a way to profit from it at the expense of American voters.

Trump Backers Fail to Convince

August 2016

Living in our liberal area is a blessing I didn't have when I lived in rural and small-town Ohio, Pennsylvania, and West Virginia. Here, the biggest political argument is Bernie versus Hillary, so I know I'm among my tribe. But I also make sure to stay connected to conservatives through personal relationships, social media, and information outlets. Being in a bubble is like binging on Boston cream donuts: comforting, but not good for us.

Instead of dismissing Donald Trump's supporters, I've been reaching out to my conservative friends to see why they support a candidate who projects the opposite of traditional American values. The results are revealing.

Many of them don't "support" Trump so much as they hate Hillary Clinton. They honestly believe the fictions of their right-wing bubble: that Clinton killed Americans in Benghazi, committed treason by email, and should be in jail. They can't provide evidence for these beliefs, but they continue to claim that Trump, despite his obvious faults, trumps Clinton.

I strongly support Clinton and can name dozens of her policy proposals, career accomplishments, and character traits that make her a great candidate. But when I ask for positive reasons to support Trump, things get weird.

My conservative friends almost always begin with, "Trump speaks his mind." He certainly does—that's the problem. When I ask how Trump's rejection of "political correctness" and multiple profane remarks, nasty insults, and outright lies are acceptable, they deflect. When I ask if rudeness and bullying are strong presidential qualifications, they attack Clinton.

I send my friends to the most respected political fact-checker, PolitiFact.com, for a comparison of Clinton and Trump. Clinton is among the most honest politicians they've ever rated, and Trump is one of the biggest liars. "No," I assure my Republican friends, "PolitiFact isn't an agenda-driven political operation. That's Fox News."

Another reason they support Trump is that "we need a businessman in the White House." Really? Have they heard of George W.

Bush and Herbert Hoover? We tried businessmen in the White House, and the results were depressing—literally.

Trump's businesses aren't really something to boast about—although boast, he does. Trump brags about using multiple bankruptcies to make money, usually by screwing everyone else. As Clinton said recently, "How can anybody lose money running a casino?" Fellow rich guy Michael Bloomberg said, "Trump says he wants to run the nation like he's running his business. God help us!"

Trump supporters seem to forget that the business of government is people, not profit. Trump isn't as great at profit as he claims, and he's even worse at helping people.

My Republican friends claim that Trump will bring jobs back to America. "Which jobs?" I ask. "Making Trump Ties in China and Trump Suits in Mexico?" The financial research firm Moody's Analytics looked at both candidates' economic proposals and determined that Clinton would create 10.4 million American jobs, while Trump would lead to 3.5 million job losses. Moody's isn't exactly a liberal think tank filled with granola-crunching sandal wearers.

My Trump-supporting friends say that he will somehow fix political corruption. This guy has been involved in thousands of lawsuits. Worst of all, New York state court found that Trump operated Trump University without a license, and two major lawsuits are pending against the fake "university" that Trump put his name on to scam millions of dollars from thousands of people. Any claim that Trump is above corruption is absurd.

The list of bad reasons goes on.

"Trump will stop ISIS!" Trump claims to have a secret plan to defeat ISIS, but he won't reveal it unless he's elected. That's just plain nuts.

"Trump is self-funded." Nope. He solicits donations.

"Trump will take care of our veterans." He stiffed veterans' organizations on charitable donations until reporters shamed him.

"Trump won't hide things like those evil Clintons." He won't even release his tax returns, something every other major candidate does.

"Trump will surround himself with great advisors." His campaign staff and surrogates are an embarrassment.

"Trump will dump Obamacare." And with no coherent plan to take its place, twenty million people will lose coverage and the insurance companies will go back to their abusive practices unchecked.

"Trump will reverse Obama's terrible policies." The policies that cut unemployment and the federal budget deficit in half? We'll keep those, thanks.

"Trump will make other countries fear us." They're already laughing at us for even considering Trump.

"Trump will save us from Muslims who hate America." Like Ghazala, Khizr, and Humayun Khan? They are what America stands for.

"Trump will build a wall and close our open borders." Illegal immigration is down under Obama. Look it up!

"Trump's a winner!" Then why is he already acting like a loser by claiming that the debates and the election are rigged against him?

All this fuzzy-headed trumpery is almost enough to make me climb into that liberal bubble and binge on those donuts. But I won't.

Liberalism means keeping an open mind—open even to my conservative friends who haven't yet provided good reasons to support Trump. But they'll keep trying. Like their candidate himself, what they lack in common sense, they try to make up for in persistence.

One Hundred Reasons to Vote for Hillary Clinton

September 2016

A Republican friend dared me to name five reasons to support Hillary Clinton without mentioning Donald Trump. Challenge accepted—times twenty! Here are one hundred reasons from Clinton's background, character, and views that make her worthy of our enthusiastic support.

Clinton grew up in a middle-class family (1) with Republican parents, but she was wise enough to become a Democrat in college (2), supporting anti-war liberal Eugene McCarthy for president in 1968 (3) and remaining a progressive Democrat her whole life (4).

She earned a degree in political science from Wellesley (5), writing her thesis on poverty and community development (6). She was student government president (7) and honored as student commencement speaker (8).

She then studied law at Yale (9), serving on the law review board (10). During law school, she went undercover to investigate racial segregation in Alabama schools (11), part of her career-long commitment to battling racism (12). After graduating, she studied at Yale's Child Study Center (13) where she wrote a groundbreaking report on children's rights published in the Harvard Educational Review (14).

As a young lawyer, she co-founded Arkansas Advocates for Children and Families (15), directed the Arkansas Legal Aid Clinic (16), chaired the Legal Services Corporation (17), and chaired the American Bar Association's Commission on Women in the Profession (18). She was twice named by the National Law Journal as one of the most influential lawyers in America (19).

As First Lady of Arkansas (20), she championed Arkansas's Home Instruction Program for Preschool Youth (21), chaired the Arkansas Educational Standards Committee (22), worked with the Arkansas Advocates for Children and Families (23), and served on the board of the Arkansas Children's Hospital Legal Services (24) and the Children's Defense Fund (25).

As First Lady of the United States (26), she chaired the President's Task Force on Health Care Reform (27) and worked across political divisions to help pass the Children's Health Insurance

Program (28), the Adoption and Safe Families Act (29), and the Foster Care Independence Act (30). She famously advocated for women's rights in China (31) and wrote a bestselling book about parenting (32) while parenting her daughter in the White House (33).

During eight years in the Senate (34), she learned the legislative process first-hand (35) while working on numerous committees (36) She advocated for 9-11 first-responders (37), rural broadband (38), veterans' health care (39), public schools (40), and clean energy (41), among many other significant efforts (42).

President Obama chose her for Secretary of State (43), and she aided him in vastly improving America's standing in the world (44). She continued to champion the rights of women (45) and impoverished people (46) around the world. As America's chief diplomat (47), she combined toughness (48) with a philosophy of using military power only as a last resort (49). Her many other accomplishments included being part of the effort to get Osama bin Laden (50) and laying the groundwork for the Iran nuclear deal (51).

Her work with the Clinton Foundation helped millions of people worldwide (52). She and her family didn't get a penny from the foundation (53) and, in fact, donated millions of their own earnings to help others (54). And no foundation donors got special benefits from her while she was Secretary of State (55), despite her detractors' false claims.

In her current campaign, Clinton has held hundreds of town halls (56) focused on listening to (57) and learning from (58) the public. She doesn't demonize anyone's ethnic background (59) or belittle her opponents (60), but she isn't afraid to call out those who purposely appeal to intolerance (61). Fact-checkers consistently rate her one of the most honest candidates (62). Despite countless lies told about her (63), she doesn't lie about her opponents (64).

She frequently says, "America already is great" (65). Basing a campaign on optimism (66) is far better than exploiting negativity and cynicism (67). Clinton's campaign can be summed up by one comment to an undecided voter at a town hall: "Whether you end up supporting me or not, I will support you" (68).

Clinton has specific proposals on many issues that will improve the lives of everyday Americans: minimum wage (69), voting rights (70), unions (71), campaign finance reform (72), Wall Street reform (73), LGBTQ equality (74), religious freedom (75), gun-safety regulation (76), equal pay (77), college affordability (78), universal pre-K

(79), taxes (80), jobs (81), diplomacy over war (82), reproductive choice (83), criminal justice reform (84), universal health care (85), Social Security (86), Medicare (87), stem cell research (88), immigration (89), veterans support (90), climate change (91), clean energy (92), and a host of other important issues (93).

This list dumbfounded my Republican friend. Republicans have propagandized Clinton for thirty-plus years because they know they can't beat her in an honest campaign (94).

Some people will read this column and still hate Clinton. But that won't stop her from serving our country (95). She'll handle the attacks with strength (96) grace (97), and without cynicism (98).

The bottom line is that the people who know Hillary Clinton best admire her most (99). The people who criticize her most, by contrast, know almost nothing about her (100).

The 2016 Election Complaint Department

October 2016

Election Quality Engineer: Welcome to the 2016 Election Complaint Department. How may I help you?

Disgruntled Voter: I'm an undecided voter with some complaints. First of all, we have such awful candidates. Trump and Clinton are both horrible.

Election Quality Engineer: We've heard that complaint from many disgruntled voters recently. But the facts show that only one candidate is actually awful. One has a long history of questionable and possibly illegal business practices, a rude demeanor, possibly racist views, clearly misogynist tendencies, very little knowledge of the issues, no government experience, and a propensity for lying and then claiming that the system is rigged whenever his lies are called out. The other is Hillary Clinton.

Disgruntled Voter: Yeah, sure, Trump's terrible. Everybody knows that. But Hillary isn't any better. I saw on the internet that she's a criminal who murders her enemies and ran a fake charity and sold top-secret e-mails to the Soviet Union.

Election Quality Engineer: The internet is filled with many psychologically disturbed people who make claims with no connection with reality. That's what these attacks on Clinton are. Meanwhile, back in reality, she has never been arrested or even seriously suspected of any crime. She never sent or received e-mail messages properly marked as classified in private e-mails. Her family foundation is a real charity that helps millions of people around the world. Clinton is actually a well-respected public servant with decades of experience and countless accomplishments who has been relentlessly attacked by people who oppose her. Also, the Soviet Union dissolved a quarter of a century ago.

Disgruntled Voter: But isn't Hillary just as rude as Trump? Didn't she call his supporters "deportable"?

Election Quality Engineer: She called half of his supporters "deplorable." But she also said that many of his supporters are frustrated with their economic condition and deserve our empathy. Surveys show that 65% of Trump supporters think President Obama is a Muslim, 59% believe he wasn't born in the U.S., 49% believe Blacks are more violent than Whites, 40% believe Blacks are lazier than Whites, 31% believe gay people shouldn't be allowed into the U.S., and 20% believe Lincoln shouldn't have freed the slaves. That's clearly "deplorable" and borderline "deportable."

Disgruntled Voter: So, isn't Hillary so old and sick that she almost died last month? Maybe we should replace her with Bernie Sanders.

Election Quality Engineer: Clinton is actually younger than both Trump and Sanders. She had a brief battle with pneumonia recently and showed remarkable strength to campaign while she was sick, but she eventually took a couple of days off. When you call in sick, does your employer replace you with the less-qualified person who you beat out for the job? I hope not. Clinton looked far more energetic and healthy than Trump at their recent debates.

Disgruntled Voter: Yeah, I saw those debates. I heard that Hillary had an earpiece so she could get answers piped directly into her brain and used hand signals to communicate with the moderator and ordered Trump's microphone cut off so no one could hear him. What's up with that?

Election Quality Engineer: The earpiece and hand-signal conspiracies come from the same pitiful people who believe she's a murderer. And Trump's microphone seemed to be working well enough that we heard him interrupt Clinton multiple times, lie repeatedly, and sniffle more often than a sickly toddler.

Disgruntled Voter: Doesn't Clinton own all those fact-check thingies? That's why they pick on Trump so much.

Election Quality Engineer: The fact-checkers who called out Trump's many debate lies are nonpartisan information services. They "pick on" Trump because he lied about ten times as often as Clinton did in the debate. All politicians stretch the truth, but Trump lives on another planet.

Disgruntled Voter: Trump must have said something right because he won all of those post-debate polls, didn't he?

Election Quality Engineer: Those "polls" are actually just online surveys that allow anyone to vote, often multiple times. Right-wing activists have a long history of flooding these surveys to promote a dishonest narrative. In the polls conducted using reliable methods that yield accurate results, Clinton beat Trump like a dusty rug.

Disgruntled Voter: Oh, come on. Trump can't be that bad.

Election Quality Engineer: Well, just recently we've learned that Trump may have violated the Cuban embargo, had dealings with a bank that supports terrorists in Iran, was exposed for his racist "birther" lies, attempted to fat-shame and slut-shame a former Miss Universe, tweeted about a sex tape in the wee hours of the morning, used his foundation as a personal and campaign slush fund, implied that veterans with PTSD aren't "strong," lost nearly a billion dollars in one year, may not have paid federal income tax for many years, and questioned Hillary Clinton's marriage even though he has bragged about his multiple infidelities in his multiple marriages.

Disgruntled Voter: Okay, I see your point.

Election Quality Engineer: So, what was your original complaint? Something about Trump and Clinton being equally bad?

Disgruntled Voter: Never mind. I've decided to do the only sane thing. I'm voting for Hillary.

Trump's Concession Speech (in a Better World)

November 2016

Author's Note: I wrote this fictionalized speech on election day 2016 as I prepared for Donald Trump to be his typically idiotic self after he lost the election. Unfortunately, he managed an Electoral College fluke to gain office. This column became the basis for my book, Donald Trump's Top Secret Concession Speech, a satire that explored hat it would be like if Trump had a conscience. Unfortunately, he has proven again and again that he doesn't. I still believe that somewhere in a better world, he lost.

My fellow Americans, I lost, fair and square. This has forced me to do some soul searching. I haven't found one yet, but I'll keep looking because I've got nothing better to do.

My fellow Americans, I'm sorry.

Last week, my staff took away my access to Twitter, so I've had time to think for the first time in many months. I found this internet thingie and Goobled myself instead of tweeting insults at all hours of the night.

I didn't like what I saw. I've been appealing to hate and fear and jealousy and bigotry and sexism. I'm sorry for all that. Did you know the KKK endorsed me? How could anyone vote for me after that? I said that we should kill the families of suspected terrorists, which I learned is a war crime. What's wrong with me?

I said that women should be punished for abortions, as if I have any right to tell them what to do. I'm sorry. I said I'd get rid of gay marriage. I don't even know if I believe that, or if I just said it to get homophobes to vote for me. Either way, I'm sorry.

I even looked at my own website. Who wrote that garbage? Why am I trying to give rich people like me another tax break when there are hungry children in the country? Why do I claim that I'll be strong against terrorism when I'm so terrified that I want to hide the whole country behind a wall?

Do you know they have fact-checkers on the internet? Why didn't anyone tell me that I was lying so much? I was mostly just making up crap and repeating crap from my advisors. Why would anyone believe all that crap and vote for me?

I'm sorry for misusing your anger to run for office. I knew your anger should be directed toward wealthy jerks like me who put my greed above the good of the country. I'm sorry I tried to blame problems people like me created on people who have been trying to help.

If I had any decency, I would have encouraged Americans to direct their anger toward the greedy people who have squeezed the life out of the American middle class. But I was one of those greedy people who rigged the system against you. Hell, I go on trial for fraud in a few weeks because of my fake university, and my fake foundation will probably be next. I'm sorry for being a con artist.

I'm sorry for being a weakling who thought that treating women like objects made me a big man. I'm sorry for not really understanding that women are real people and not just things to grab. I'm sorry for cheating on all of my wives and then pandering to born-again Christians. What's wrong with me?

Just so everybody knows, this isn't a fake apology like the one my staff wrote for me after that tape of me bragging about sexual assault went public. This apology is real. I won't use this apology to blame other people. For once in my life, I'm going to try to accept responsibility.

I'm sorry that I attacked President Obama and Hillary Clinton. I acted like a terrible person during this campaign. Am I a terrible person? I don't know. I've been so busy fantasizing about ruling the world that I've never really thought about my own behavior. I sure as hell seem like a terrible person when I watch myself in those debates. What kind of person shouts "Wrong!" when someone else is talking? A terrible person, that's who. I'm sorry for acting like a spoiled toddler.

I'm sorry I treated Hillary like she's a terrible person. Have you people actually ever listened to Hillary? She's way smarter than I am. She knows what she's doing. She actually has plans—good ones! I looked them up. You should too. She makes sense. I never had plans. All I had were stupid walls and stupid slogans on stupid hats. Smart people have made me feel stupid my whole life. I've obviously been bragging about how smart I am because I feel stupid inside. I hope it's not too late to change.

Hillary actually is a good person. She's the opposite of "nasty." She's not a criminal. She cares way more about making America great than I ever did. Every time I called her "Crooked Hillary," I was just hoping that no one would notice how crooked I've always been. I'm sorry.

Hillary will be a great president. You'll see. I'm glad more people voted for her than for me. American already is great, and she'll help keep it great if you give her a chance and don't listen to ignorant blowhards like me.

I'm going to go away now and shut my big fat mouth for a long time. It's like the old joke about the guy who wouldn't want to join a club that would have him as a member. I wouldn't want to be president of a country stupid enough to elect me president.

Running for Safety in an Unsafe Age

December 2016

On a recent cold but sunny Sunday morning, my wife Betsy and I hunted through some drawers to find eight small safety pins to attach our numbers for the Hot Chocolate Run for Safe Passage. Betsy and I love supporting our local anti-domestic violence organization even more than we love running through the streets of our hometown.

Safe Passage gives hope to people in the seemingly hopeless situation of domestic violence. The Hot Chocolate Run is a joyful, exuberant event where thousands of people come together to turn hope into tangible fundraising that helps create a safer world.

We were short by one pin, so I took one from the lapel of the sport coat I planned to wear to work the following day. As a teacher, I've had a difficult time bringing hope to my classrooms since our country elected Donald Trump. Facilitating coherent discussions for angry, frightened students hasn't been easy.

Leading up to the election, our work with writing and communications had focused on supporting claims with facts and evidence, as well as maintaining civility rather than vitriol. Now I face these students after the candidate who ran the most fact-free, evidence-deficient campaign in history has won the election. The candidate who ran the most offensive campaign since George Wallace somehow convinced more than sixty million voters to affirm his attacks with their votes.

How safe are we in a nation whose president-elect graces our Twitter feed with outright lies about election fraud and juvenile screeds against television shows that parody him? Are we safe in a nation whose new leader seems intent on conducting domestic and foreign affairs in ways that maximize his personal profit? Are we safe in a nation whose potential cabinet members' greed, corruption, and bigotry represent the antithesis of our best American values?

The safety pin I wear on my jacket is there to tell my students and colleagues that I'll offer "safe passage" if they feel threatened. I'll provide a listening ear or a protective ally for anyone who feels threatened by the atmosphere that led to the election of a president who rejects facts and embraces division. More than that, it tells them that I'm actively working to make our country and our world a safer place.

Wearing a pin to symbolize safety isn't new. Some reports place its origin in the Danish resistance to Nazis during WWII. More recently, safety pins have been used as signs against Islamophobia in Australia and anti-immigrant bigotry in Great Brittan. Not surprisingly, white supremacists have attempted to co-opt the safety pin by affixing it to their guns and Trump hats. Those guns and hats are a clue that safety isn't the real goal.

Some of my students and colleagues have asked me about the safety pin, and nearly all have appreciated the meaning behind the symbol. Unfortunately, some have missed the point. One Trump-supporting colleague doubted I'd be an ally to any students who had voted for Trump. "Colleges are filled with liberals," he said. "Conservative students are outnumbered and scared."

I told him that I'd definitely be an ally to any students actually being abused because they voted for Trump. But simply being asked to defend their vote with facts isn't abuse. Much of the "liberal" part of "liberal education" is a respect for evidence-based inquiry. When people don't have evidence to support their views, then the rest of us need protection from their fact-free agenda.

One of Trump's recent fact-free claims is that flag burning should be penalized with jail time or loss of citizenship. That's already been ruled unconstitutional. But his superficial rants resonate with those who think patriotism means never criticizing your country. That's not patriotism. That's nationalism, which has led to all sorts of problems—see the aforementioned WWII, for example. Patriotism means loving your country realistically enough to want to make it even better, not just ignoring its flaws. We need to guard against the nationalistic oppression that Trump and his followers embrace.

Burning the American flag, unfortunately, sets flame to the good and the bad. For folks who long for a flag to burn, they might consider the Confederate flag instead. That one symbolizes Trump's views far better than the stars and stripes. For those interested in the symbolic value of a piece of clothing, ask a Trump hatter, "What makes America great?" I still haven't gotten anything close to a good answer from them on that one. We can't normalize Trump's brand of aggressive ignorance.

The safety pin symbol is probably a fad. But actions always count more than symbols. I'll keep working for "safe passage," by plying my creaky joints in next year's Hot Chocolate Run, by standing up for anyone who is oppressed, and by continuing to focus on facts and evidence as the best way to foster civic safety.

No one knows for certain how dangerous Trump's presidency will be, but our country's best responses should be hopeful, firm, informed dissent. We must push forward with facts, evidence, and civility—no matter how often we see the opposite from the temporary resident of our White House during the next four years.

Trump Voters Work in Mysterious Ways

January 2017

Growing up, I attended a tiny Lutheran church near our family farm. During a Christmas service four decades ago, as our beloved pastor was delivering another soft-spoken sermon about kindness and grace, thick sheets of snow thundered down the pitched church roof in a seismic event that threatened to collapse our rickety house of worship.

Dust flickered through the stained glass sunlight shafts. The communal hush and the pastor's stunned expression quickly gave way to relieved laughter as we realized that God hadn't thrust his hand through that wintry roof to end our earthly existence.

Last month, my wife Betsy and I attended the Christmas Eve service at Northampton's Unitarian Society. We felt the same sense of community that drew me to the church of my youth long ago. Something else about that Christmas Eve service emanated a sense of welcome: The pews were clearly not occupied by people whose faith led them to vote for Donald Trump.

My own religious views are simple. I'm pretty sure that there's a higher power, but I wouldn't be surprised if there's not. Either way, our purpose in life seems to be making the world a better place and being kind to each other. Those views are compatible with Christian values—but not with Trumpocrisy.

White evangelical Christians voted for Trump by a five-to-one margin—"white" being the key word. Trump purposely appealed to resentment against ethnic groups who, ironically, look like the real Jesus, a dark-skinned Middle Easterner vastly different from his blue-eyed, sandy-haired, porcelain-skinned modern portraits.

Trump's life reflects Christian values about as much as those White Jesus portraits resemble the true Nazarene. Trump's hostility toward immigrants goes against basic Biblical teaching, and he'll never be mistaken for a Good Samaritan. Of the seven deadly sins, only sloth isn't on his résumé. He works hard at his pride, envy, wrath, gluttony, lust, and greed.

Trump tries to mimic the pseudo-Christian paternal authority figure, but he's more like the schoolyard bully who lashes out because he's weak and fearful. He may be a "strongman" in the dictatorial sense, but he's far from strong. Hillary Clinton is much stronger than Trump and proved so repeatedly by tattering his empty, ill-fitting suit at each debate.

According to one of my conservative Christian friends, Trump's election was "divine intervention" to protect us from Hillary Clinton. Putting aside the idea that God makes presidential endorsements, I asked what was wrong with Clinton. "Everything," he replied, "She's as bad as Hussein Obama," and then he launched into a diatribe about Obama and Clinton killing Americans in Benghazi, murdering nine-month babies in the womb, and bringing terrorists right into our homes.

He must think that God reads the same fake news that he does because none of that is true in a Ninth Commandment sense. Obama and Clinton are actually guided by their personal Christian faith. Yet right-wing Christians rant about Obama being a secret Muslim and chant that Clinton should be locked up. Does the term "Pharisees" ring a bell?

Christianity—the Jesus variety, featuring grace, social justice, and love—is consistent with liberal values. Unfortunately, the Republican Party hitched itself to the extreme anti-abortion splinter of Christianity decades ago, successfully mainstreaming fringe views. Anyone who doesn't understand how that long-con led directly to Trump's pretend piety should read the appropriately titled book, *Republican Gomorrah* by Max Blumenthal.

Trump can do no wrong for most Republican Christians. For example, Trump tweeted a Christmas photo of himself holding up his tiny fist while standing before a Christmas tree. Had Obama posed like that, Republicans would have accused him of injecting a "Black Power" symbol into his "War on Christmas."

Trump's raised fist actually mimics a gesture co-opted by White supremacists. Was Trump using his Christmas photo to dog-whistle his racist supporters? That seems absurd until we consider Trump's overwhelming support among the KKK and other racist organizations that also identify as Christian. Yet no Christian leaders condemned Trump's behavior.

Can anyone imagine Trump praying? "Thank God I was born wealthy, white, male, American, and straight." Without even one of those gifts, Trump's real estate career wouldn't have advanced beyond gossipy overnight desk clerk at an hourly-rate motel on the wrong side of the tracks.

What hymns would Trump sing? "How Great Trump Art," "Nearer My Trump to Thee," and "O Come Let Us Adore Trump" aren't real hymns—although Trump may try to use them for his inauguration if he can't blackmail any celebrities to perform.

What would a Trump sermon be like? When he spoke at right-wing Christian Liberty University, Trump mentioned Paul's Second Epistle to the Corinthians, which every Christian knows is pronounced, "Second Corinthians." But Trump said "Two Corinthians," as if introducing a bad joke: "Two Corinthians walk into a bar."

Unfortunately, the joke is on everyone. Trump, the antithesis of Christian values, will soon be president, thanks in large part to voters identified as Christians. Whether we're softly singing "Silent Night" at the Unitarian service or being conned into seeing Trump as God's president, the truth is that we're all Trump's victims. Some people will just take longer than others to learn that lesson.

Welcome to the Resistance

I woke on Friday, January 20, 2017, with a lingering head cold. Like many Americans, I feel like I woke up sick on November 9, 2016, and haven't recovered. Before that date, our country had spent many months fighting off a nasty infection, but, overnight, our defenses failed, and we picked up the worst bug we've ever had.

Our nation's current illness is similar to the Swine Flu (pun intended). But the swine flu was better because it only keeps its victim down for a couple of weeks. By contrast, we're all facing at least a four-year porcine period.

I shook off my head cold and went to work on January 20, as many millions of our neighbors around the globe do every day. When I arrived at Asnuntuck Community College in Enfield, Connecticut, my work home for a quarter of a century, I marveled at how the building had changed during our recent construction phase.

The entire front of the building is being upgraded from a traditional brick-and-mortar schoolhouse to a modern glass-and-steel facade. In particular, I noted a feature resembling a wing dramatically arching toward the sky high above the front entrance. It reminded me of something from *Star Wars*. Sometimes I imagine all this construction is actually a secret project to build a space ship. If so, January 20 was a splendid day to explore the universe in search of a better world.

As you probably know, a big event took place in Washington, DC, on January 20. I chose to go to work instead. But I had time between classes and meetings to watch the live broadcast on television. I chose not to. He wants us to watch. I refuse to give him my attention on his terms. Instead, I read the transcript later. The most positive thing I can say is that it made my head hurt only slightly more as the day progressed.

President Obama finished his term by becoming the first sitting president to publish a scholarly article in *Harvard Law Review*. Meanwhile, the new occupant of the White House began his term by addressing the nation like a toddler who needs a nap.

My wife Betsy and I finished the day on a good note by listening to Jane Yolen (a local treasure) read from her wonderful new book of political poems, *Before the Vote After*, at Easthampton's White Square Books (another local treasure). Being in the presence of people who cultivated intelligence, creativity, and empathy, among other basic American values, helped us begin to move on from that historic downer of a day.

Saturday, January 21, dawned clear and bright. I inhaled the crisp air as best my head cold would allow, and Betsy and I switched on the television to see millions—literally millions—of people worldwide marching to protest the guy who gave the previous day's terrible speech.

We drove to town and walked down the hill from Smith College toward Pulaski Park just in time to see the bright lights of a police cruiser leading our own protest march—a march that kept marching and marching, taking nearly half an hour to wind its way from beginning to end.

Betsy and I were thrilled to nestle among the three thousand souls who added to the millions speaking out—shouting out—against the angry toddler. As we lifted our voices to join those around us, our faith in humanity was renewed. My head cold may not have cleared, but some of our sense of foreboding did.

Saturday, January 21, showed me once again why I love my town and why I love my country. The protest signs we saw were smart, funny, and hopeful: "Love Trumps Hate." "Queer Jews Against Islamophobia." "Hate Won't Make Us Great." "Kindness is a Family Value." "Build Bridges for All Instead of a Wall." "May We Find Our Humanity." "Make America Think Again." "Make America Kind Again."

The most instructive sign displayed a single word: "Resist."

Sometimes, when we resist illness, we get sicker before we get better. When I actually had the Swine Flu a few years ago, it turned into pneumonia, keeping me home from work longer than any other time in my life. In a similar way, the Electoral College victor seems determined to sicken our nation more each day.

But my January head cold has faded to February sniffles. We will heal our country with a long course of many different treatments to resist the current infection.

I'm not sure exactly what this resistance will look like, but I do know that protesting in all its forms—coming together in large groups, laboring alone, plodding on, calling and writing our representatives, practicing patience, critical thinking, and humor—will each play a part. We'll resist even when we're sick and tired. In fact, we'll resist especially when we don't feel like resisting. That's the most important time.

In reality, my little community college isn't a secret spaceship being constructed for our escape. Instead, it's another way that we stay here, move forward, and work to make this planet a better, healthier place to live. That's what I'll strive for every day during at least the next four years.

Forget flying away on that spaceship. Let's stay grounded here and march together.

Satirizing Trump

March 2017

Author's Note: This essay became the "Author's Afterword" for Donald Trump's Top Secret Concession Speech, *the satirical novella I wrote in response to Trump's election.*

On Tuesday, November 8, 2016, I worked from home most of the day, grading papers, planning classes, and writing. My monthly newspaper column was due Thursday evening for Monday publication, so I set to drafting what I thought would be a reaction to Trump's election loss. I figured that he would end his run the same way he had campaigned: petty, dishonest, bitter, barely coherent, and with no sense of the damage his terrible presence in our national politics had created.

In anticipation of Trump's "concession speech" being full of lies, bluster, and accusations of a "rigged election," I wrote what I thought he should have said. I wrote an apology in his own voice as if he had finally realized that he owed the nation a massive apology.

That night, I watched in horror as Trump remained competitive in several key states even as he fell further behind in the popular vote. As the dead of night descended, Trump held on for a tiny Electoral College victory.

I barely slept that night and had to face my students the next day. I had been telling them that facts, research, critical thinking, civility, and empathy were keys to good scholarship and good citizenship. But the candidate who had violated each of those essential qualities had somehow won the presidential election. They were as depressed as I was.

I eventually added a preface to my column indicating that this fictional concession speech was set in a better world, the real world where the unimaginable remained unimaginable.

In the face of the Trump victory, my column was well received as an insightful look into the con artistry that had led to Trump's victory. The strong responses led me to start working on expanding that column into a book of Trump's fictionalized ramblings, titled, "Donald Trump's Top Secret Concession Speech." That book is now finished.

Pretty much everything in the book, despite its fictional format, is based on verifiable facts about Trump's actions, character, and campaign. The non-fact-based fictional elements I added to the book are the tiny portions of humility, humanity, and shame that I doubt he will ever actually feel.

All my life, I've written civil, scholarly, reasonable essays with some generous hints of satire. Trump's antics invite satire. Writing a book about him that is total satire wasn't that big a stretch, even if I had to stretch my writing enough to occupy Trump's big, wrinkled, lumpy, empty suit.

People have asked me if I'm afraid Trump will sue me. I'd rather he didn't, but he doesn't react well to criticism or mockery. We should all aspire to a life that would prompt Donald Trump to sue us.

Satire is free speech protected by the First Amendment, but I'm glad that I personally know an ACLU lawyer. (Hi Bill!) Most likely, Trump will never hear of this book. Reading is not one of his strong suits. I'm sure I'll get some misspelled hate mail from his most deplorable supporters. But I already get hate mail from them for my reasonable newspaper columns. Maybe I'll get one of Trump's infamous hate tweets. A guy can dream.

Our job in the age of Trump is to resist his terrible and unjust policies and not be deflated by his embarrassing character. Every day is the worst day of Trump's presidency, but we have to keep going in whatever way we can. Most days, I have no idea how to do that, but I keep trying. Most days, I cycle through the five stages of grief a dozen times in random order, but I keep trying.

The best advice I heard about how to go on during Trump's gloomy reign came from a singer I know. She said that we all have to keep doing what we do best. She needs to keep singing, as best she can, the songs that make the world a better place. She'll keep singing progressive, loving songs that combat Trump's regressive, cruel agenda. And she'll also sing songs that challenge Trump directly and open our nation's eyes to the ways that Trump violates the values that have actually made America great.

I'll keep teaching my students that critical thinking, evidence, creativity, and empathy are the keys to learning, growing, and being the best citizens they can be.

I'm a terrible singer, so I'll keep writing. That's one of the things I do best. I'll keep writing my civil, empathetic, and reasonable commentaries about politics and current events. And I'll keep writing gentle and not-so-gentle satire when people like Trump deserve it—which is often.

My grandchildren are one and three years old right now. Many years from now in better times, they'll ask me, "Grampy, what did you do to resist Trump?" And I'll be able to tell them, "I wrote a funny book to help people see how horrible Trump was, and the book also gave them a little hope and something to laugh about in a very sad period in history." And my sweet and smart grandkids will be proud of their old Grampy.

And America will be great again because we resisted Trump.

This Trump Disaster Should Have Been Avoided

April 2017

I recently asked a friend of mine at work who voted for Donald Trump, "Any regrets?"

He looked at the floor and muttered, "Trump isn't what I expected." As he retreated down the hallway, he called back, "But Hillary would have been worse." His shaky voice confirmed that even he didn't believe his words.

Before the election, my friend always gave me the same two reasons for supporting Trump: Trump knows what he's doing, and Hillary would be worse. He definitely regrets the first reason, and he's reconsidering the second as well.

Let's look at our current Trump debacle and imagine a Clinton presidency instead.

Trump has set new records for delusional bragging, being a sore winner, and embarrassing the country. He lies about voter fraud being the reason he lost the popular vote. He lies about the size of his inauguration crowd. He lies about Obama spying on him. He bad-mouths the millions of protestors who question his policies and character. He holds campaign rallies only in states he won while embracing policies that he admits will harm his supporters. He insults anyone who questions him every chance he gets.

Had Clinton won, she would have based her policies on values that bring us together. She would have looked for common ground with any Republicans interested in serving the nation rather than playing partisan politics. She would have listened to the voters who didn't choose her and worked for policies to help them, even as they slander her.

Trump's administrative picks have been a weird array of family members, extremists, incompetents, saboteurs, and corporate cronies. He appointed a paid agent of foreign dictators as his National Security Advisor and the head of an "Alt-Right" (translations: White Supremacist) website as his Chief Strategist. Instead of "draining the swamp," as he promised, Trump made himself King of the Swamp.

Clinton would have selected accomplished specialists with a rich history of public service for her administration. And they would have represented America's diversity instead of reflecting a percentage of white males that rivals *Duck Dynasty's* regular viewers.

Trump has repeatedly denied Russia's attack on our election—even as members of his inner circle are implicated, and Trump's compromising business ties to Russia are revealed. Trump refuses to condemn Vladimir Putin as he murders his political opponents, oppresses his people, and leads a criminal Kleptocracy.

Clinton would have called for independent investigations into Russia's subversion of our election to prevent future attacks. She would have led the free world's opposition to Putin's dictatorial reign, just as she helped Obama do as his Secretary of State.

Without sufficient intelligence, Trump approved a misguided military raid in Yemen that led to multiple civilian casualties, little useful information recovery, and the death of an American Navy Seal. Benghazi pales by comparison.

Clinton would have shown restraint, resolve, and respect for our military and intelligence communities. She would have personally overseen missions in the Situation Room instead tweeting, as Trump did during his tragic Yemen raid.

Trump repeatedly embarrasses our country with obnoxious tweets, interviews, press conferences, and meetings with world leaders. Clinton would have represented us with strength, class, and dignity—just as she always has.

Trump signed Republican bills damaging our online privacy, allowing coal-mining waste to be dumped into rivers, and making it easier for mentally ill people to get guns. Clinton would have vetoed such nonsense.

Trump keeps pushing for misguided mass deportations and a wall that Mexico will not pay for. Clinton would have pushed for comprehensive, common-sense immigration reform.
Trump issued illegal, offensive travel bans for majority-Muslim countries, making America less safe by advancing the false narrative that we hate Muslims. Clinton would have made it clear, as Obama and even George W. Bush did, that our nation is not at war with Islam.

Trump's budget attacks the poor, education, diplomacy, and every aspect of American culture not related to defense contractors and corporations. Clinton would have budgeted with true

American values and progressive initiatives to fund real efforts to keep America great.

Trump nominated a Supreme Court pick with a record of attacking the rights of women, workers, and disabled people. Clinton would have renominated Obama's well-respected pick, Merrick Garland, who was unconstitutionally blocked by cynical Republicans, or she would have nominated someone even better—perhaps Obama himself.

Trump tried to rush through a senseless Obamacare repeal. Clinton would have studied the issues, brought all sides into the discussion, deliberated with care, and championed real reforms to improve Obamacare and lay the groundwork for an eventual single-payer system.

In retrospect, how could we have predicted Trump's complete incompetence? If only we had some clue during the campaign that Clinton would have been a far better president than Trump. Oh, wait. We did. The entire campaign showed that glaring contrast. Some people just refused to see the obvious. But at least my formerly pro-Trump work friend is beginning to realize his mistake. Baby steps.

Anyone who still believes that Clinton would have been as bad as Trump is profoundly confused. His holdout followers are either hapless victims of Trump's propaganda operation or willing participants in that machine. Either way, as the world suffers under Trump, we all suffer together.

Envisioning Trump's Legacy for Humanity

May 2017

When students arrive for the first day of my creative writing class, they have a range of expectations. Many legitimately want to write, to reach across the void with words. Some simply want to check the "arts" box on their degree requirements. A few assume they can toss some flowery sentences together the night before assignments are due and get an easy A. Spoiler alert: That won't work.

To calibrate our viewpoint at the beginning of the semester, I ask them to join me in a speculative thought experiment.

"Don't think of your writing in this class as a throwaway, play-school assignment," I tell them. "Instead, imagine that the earth will be destroyed by plague or disaster or war just after our course ends in a few months."

Eyebrows rise around the room.

"Imagine that extra-terrestrial explorers stumble upon our little planet millions of years later. As their ship hovers above our decimated world, their archaeologists unearth the only surviving evidence that intelligent life once thrived here. All the aliens can find is the writing produced by our class. Imagine that our poems, stories, and essays represent the whole of human history and experience."

Eyes widen beneath those raised brows.

"What do you want these future aliens to think of humanity when they decipher our words?

I ask my students to consider this question as they lean into the glow of their laptops late at night or rise at dawn to revise a few lines in their old-school notebooks before the electric hum of their high-tech day begins. I hope they'll think of their writing as a contribution to human culture. Each time a new assignment deadline approaches, I remind them that our future alien friends are depending on them.

Let's apply that particular thought experiment to another scenario: What would those aliens think of our world if their discoveries were limited to this blink in time while Trump is president?

If those aliens have eyes, how will they see us? If they have noses, how will the Trump years smell to them? Will they recoil at his countless insults and attacks? If they have an advanced sense of social responsibility, what will they make of his policies that enrich the wealthy and deprive the rest?

If those aliens have a "God," will they ask why the most publicly religious among us ignored and excused Trump's obvious violations of every scripture? If they're atheist aliens who decipher right from wrong by personal morality rather than doctrine, will Trump's self-aggrandizing ways mystify them? What about his adultery and porn-star payoffs? Do these aliens have adultery and porn stars? Trump certainly does. What will they make of his disdain for the rule of law as he calls for the jailing of political opponents and those investigating his own wrongdoing?

Will these be reality-based aliens whose policies grow from facts rather than fantasy agendas? If so, what will they think of the millions of humans who believe Trump's torrential exaggerations, flip-flops, and lies? Will they think we're stupid, ignorant, misinformed, or simply primitive?

If these aliens have neighbors, will they wall themselves off from them? Or will they reach out across the expanse because they recognize that what divides us is microscopic compared with the cosmic connections among all beings? What will they think of Trump's treaty violations and threats to other countries? How will they judge a leader who encourages his followers to fear everyone different? What will they think of those followers who let that leader fan their fear into flames of hate?

Sadly, Trump and his enablers would make these aliens think that humanity was a gang of selfish, crude, dishonest, spiteful, faithless hypocrites. They'd be glad they missed us by a few million years. I'd rather we pass into oblivion than leave Trumpism as our only legacy.

Fortunately, the aliens would also find some who represented what is best about we poor human creatures. When faced with Trump, many among us have stood firm to oppose his degradations. In fact, the aliens will discover that our planet's resisters outnumbered those who acquiesced or facilitated Trumpism as surely as our anti-Trump marches dwarfed his spotty inauguration crowd.

Maybe we don't always show our best qualities as we resist. At times we curse and rant and froth. Our anger and sadness frequently overcome our sympathy for those tangled in Trump's web. But our alien friends would see that we most often keep our vision focused on the shared values of our nation and our humanity. We try our best to leave an honorable legacy.

I hope this thought experiment never becomes reality. While a visit from alien friends might be nice, I hope the encounter doesn't come at the cost of our world destroyed—or even tarnished by a leader who doesn't represent us at our best.

My students thrill me each semester with the tales they tell to represent our world, full of hope and humor and love and mystery and decency. Those aliens would find evidence that humanity as a whole is far better than the worst we've shown during the Trump years. They'd find some gems.

Education is About What's Real

June 2017

Author's Note: For the third time in my career at Asnuntuck Community College, I had the honor of delivering a brief "Greetings from the Faculty" speech at our recent commencement. My column this month is the text of that speech.

When presenting a "Greetings from the Faculty" speech, it's tempting just to say, "Greetings, everyone!" and then sit back down. This is a long ceremony, after all. But that would be fake. You've worked too hard to get here tonight. You deserve better than a fake speech. You deserve something real.

I'd like to begin with a real quote from a commencement speech just one short year ago. President Barack Obama said to the graduating class at Rutgers University, "Ignorance is not a virtue. It's not cool to not know what you're talking about."

It's fashionable these days to say that formal education isn't part of the "real world," to imply that your experience at Asnuntuck is somehow less real compared with the world outside our college classrooms, labs, hallways, and social spaces. That's just not true. Of course, the world outside formal education is a great teacher as well, but your work here has been far from fake.

Let's talk about the virtue of some real moments that real students in tonight's graduating class have shared with me regarding their time at Asnuntuck.

One student told me about a moment when his instructor kept going on and on about something called "critical thinking"—the skill of actively and objectively analyzing and evaluating the subject matter of your studies. Meanwhile, this student was innocently trying to memorize some facts and concepts that he thought might be on the midterm exam. But suddenly he saw how some of those facts fit like matching puzzle pieces with the concepts in a class he took last year that he thought he had forgotten, and those connections exploded like fireworks in his mind.

That's the result of critical thinking—that exhilarating mental explosion when he saw connections he didn't know existed. That's not fake. That's real.

Another student told me about a time last fall when she overheard friends arguing about the claims of ... well ... let's just call this person, "a famous politician." She visited the fact-checking websites her professors had told her about and searched the scholarly databases our Asnuntuck librarians suggested, and she discovered that the famous politician's claims were more fake than the plastic ferns at her dentist's office, and she felt like an engaged citizen for the first time in her life.

Her basic research with credible sources, an open mind, and without a preconceived agenda led her to base her vote not on fantasy or fear but on verifiable facts. That's not fake. That's real.

Critical thinking and basic research skills are admirable and necessary on their own, but the best education is about developing into fully rounded human beings. So when some students in tonight's graduating class saw some of their fellow students missing meals while attending multiple classes and studying and writing papers, they combined empathy with critical thinking and research to discover that food insecurity is a major reason that community college students struggle. So they got together and created the Asnuntuck Food Pantry to help feed hungry students during their days on campus.

The Food Pantry is one of the most beautiful and touching and loving student projects I've seen during the quarter of a century I've been teaching at Asnuntuck. That's not fake. That's real.

Human beings need food and water. We need air and sunshine. We need love and kindness and empathy, and we need critical thinking and basic research skills. What our planet needs more than anything right now is educated, engaged citizens who understand that we're all in this life together. We need people who can think and research and who can apply what we've learned to help each other and to make this world a better place.

Nothing about your work at Asnuntuck is fake. Your education here will be real for the rest of your life. You made this real. The admiration all of your faculty members have for all of tonight's graduates and your loved ones is very much real.

So ... greetings, everyone. Greetings and congratulations.

I'd like to finish with another quote, this one from a great contemporary philosopher. The Most Interesting Man in the World says, "Stay thirsty, my friends." On the surface, he's just trying to sell us all some beer. But on a deeper level, just like President Obama, he's telling us *not* to stay thirsty for what's fake, *not* to stay thirsty for ignorance.

Instead, stay thirsty, my friends, for the virtue of what's real.

Mark Meunier's Life of Art and Inspiration

July 2017

Not long after my wife Betsy and I began dating more than a decade ago, I met Betsy's dear friend and coworker, Trish. Soon Trish began dating her future spouse as well, a painter named Mark, and we made arrangements to meet at his home for dinner.

I worked as a housepainter to help pay my way through college long ago. The painters I knew were hard workers with great humor and storytelling skills to help pass the long hours brushing, spraying, and rolling. So I looked forward to meeting this painter named Mark.

Imagine my surprise when we met for dinner, and I discovered that the stunning artworks on the walls were Mark's creations. I kept my little bout of "painter" confusion to myself.

I've been honored to be friends with the outstanding local artist Mark Meunier since then, and I grieve his recent death after an extended illness. In many ways, Mark is a role model for my own life.

Mark and Trish have a contemplative little Buddha statue in their yard. I snapped a photo of it that I keep handy as a reminder that we all need perspective on the turmoil of politics to recharge our spirits. In the same way, Mark's life reminds me of the transformative power of art.

Mark's landscape, forests, seascapes, and botanicals call us to be stewards of the environment and appreciate more deeply just how beautiful each glance at the world can be. Mark's famous barns recall "simpler times" and remind me of my youth growing up on a small farm. His recent paintings of cupcakes and pastries help us all chuckle at how creatively human beings cultivate our sweet tooth.

Mark also inspires me to pursue my own art as I photograph my dog rollicking on the Cape Cod beaches that grace some of Mark's best paintings. Or I can write a children's poem that twists a rhyme into a shape that will delight my grandchildren or craft a short story that might give a friend insight into our inevitable aging process.

Mark's life and art are profound examples that the world is far more than the depressing place it sometimes seems as Republicans in Congress try to wrest health insurance from our most vulnerable citizens while the temporary occupant of the White House embarrasses our country on an hourly basis. Even with these problems, good people like Mark and Trish and Betsy make this a great country.

Despite his illness, Mark made it to the polls last November. He and Trish were early Bernie Sanders supporters who had the good sense to vote for Hillary Clinton in the general election. I wish more people had followed their example.

When Trish and Mark prepared to sell their house, Betsy and I helped with some chores as Mark's illness kept him from the physical work he enjoyed. While Betsy worked with Trish inside, I raked leaves and cleared brush outside.

That evening, as Mark grilled for us on the back porch, I was struck by a bright image on the mantle above their fireplace. Mark had covered the surface of a small piece of wooden building material with the same luminous gold that graced many of the frames he handcrafted for his larger paintings. Slightly below center in the gold background, a simple winter glove with a blue snowflake pattern dangled from a clothespin.

At first, I assumed this was a preliminary study for a detail in a larger painting. But a closer look revealed much more.

As a consummate realist, Mark had rendered the glove faithfully, right down to its mottled fingertips, microscopic flyaway fibers, and intricate stitching. I could almost lift it from the board and slip it over my fingers. When I held my hand near the image, I realized the glove would fit. And, like Mark's most elaborate realistic works, this simple painting went well beyond just a two-dimensional reproduction of reality.

The material itself—a discarded scrap of particle board—transformed something seemingly insignificant into a beautiful artifact. The glove he depicted held the warmth of the hand recently protected within. The snowflake pattern whimsically nodded to our human impulse to make art from even our simplest technology. The clothespin supported the glove just as we all nurture each other. The glowing background brightened the future, whatever our destiny may be.

When Mark noticed me staring, I tried not to sound like a total fanboy as I told him how much I liked the painting. He nodded, smiled, and thanked me. A few days later, Trish brought the painting to work and gave it to Betsy. On the back, Mark had written, "For Betsy and John and their helping hand."

Mark's generosity, both as an artist and a person, is a quality we all deeply need as we resist the regressive political forces impeding our nation today. I'll be reminded of Mark every time I see that glove, now prominently displayed on the mantle above our fireplace, and I'll strive to emulate his generosity in all that I do.

Everyone who knew Mark will miss him. But his life and art have made the world a better place.

Democrats Are More than Just Anti-Trump

August 2017

I just got my "Official Resistance Membership Card!" I guess I can kiss my Trump presidential pardon goodbye!

Actually, I got a letter from the Democratic Party thanking me for a recent contribution. Along with the letter was that "membership card," a wallet-sized reminder listing what my contribution supports: affordable healthcare, reliable Social Security, clean air, clean water, healthy planet, reproductive freedom, and civil rights.

It's a small card, but I'd add quite a few values of the Democratic Party (in no particular order): minimum wage increases, voting rights, unions, campaign finance reform, Wall Street reform, LGBT rights, religious freedom, freedom of the press, gun-safety regulation, equal pay, infrastructure and manufacturing support, college affordability, education funding and reform, arts funding, fair tax systems, jobs and job-training programs, diplomacy over war, criminal justice reform, drug law reform, support for Medicaid and Medicare, promotion of small business over corporations, a strong social safety net, support for veterans, comprehensive immigration reform, health and safety regulations, funding for medical research, conversion to clean/green energy, and reality-based policies.

That's a substantial list, far longer than Trump's jingoistic, four-word slogan. Democrats aren't skilled at fitting our ideas onto the front of a cap.

Ironically, despite the conventional punditry that says Democrats don't stand for anything except Trump resistance, the Democratic Party positions are readily available to anyone who reads beyond hats or bumper stickers. All a voter has to do is go to the party's website or read the official platform or listen to nearly every Democratic office-holder in the country or recall former Democratic President Barack Obama or our most recent Democratic presidential nominee. Heck, just visit Hillary Clinton's campaign website, which is still a blueprint for moving the country in a liberal, progressive, "Big-D-Democratic" direction.

Last year, when my Republican friends told me that Clinton was a power-hungry criminal who would destroy America, I always asked if they knew her positions on the issues. They usually

49

responded by claiming she wanted to abort children minutes before birth and take away everyone's guns.

That's malarkey, of course. My Republican friends got their information from right-wing websites, Fox News, and viral memes propagated by the Trump campaign and Russian spammers. I directed these friends to Clinton's website, but they refused to because they said they already knew everything about her. They didn't.

Unfortunately, a significant minority of my liberal friends refused to vote for Clinton because they were convinced that she was a closet Republican who cheated to win the nomination and was just as bad as Trump. More malarkey, some of it from those same Russians, as we've now discovered.

I also asked them if they had visited Clinton's website to evaluate her views and proposals. Few had. I asked if they agreed with liberal hero Bernie Sanders's eventual endorsement of Clinton. Most said it didn't matter. They claimed to know all they needed to know and would never vote for Clinton. Most regret that decision now.

As a communications professional, I understand that the meaning of a message resides more in what's received than transmitted. Yes, Democrats need better messaging of our values. But we have metric tons of Republican misinformation, extreme Gerrymandering, and Trumpitude to battle, so messaging isn't easy. I'll keep shouting our platform with my increasingly hoarse voice and keep hoping the party's bigwigs are working on strategies to connect with enough voters to win Congress in 2018 and the Electoral College (not just the popular vote) in 2020.

Polls show that Americans don't much like either major party these days. But those same polls also show that Americans support the positions, ideas, and values of the Democratic Party far more than those of the Republican Party. Our challenge as Democrats is to help our fellow Americans move beyond party objections and focus on the issues. Republicans are thrilled when Americans ignore issues and blame both parties because that shifts the blame away from their party's frequent rejection of common sense, equality, justice, opportunity, and basic American ideals.

A recent Washington Post/ABC poll showed that 52% of Americans think the Democratic Party "just stands against Trump," while only 37% believe we "stand for something." Pundits hitched this poll to their narrative that Democrats are only anti-Trump obstructionists, a flawed analysis of an incomplete poll question. Clearly, "standing against Trump" and "standing for something" aren't mutually exclusive. Most Democrats I know would join me in both camps.

Yes, I want to resist Trump because he's probably the most inappropriate person ever to inhabit the White House. Beyond his repugnant character, Trump is working against pretty much every liberal/progressive/Democratic initiative that has actually made America great as we continue to work toward "a more perfect union."

As much as I resist Trump and his enablers with my full patriotic spirit, that's not the only reason I'm a Democrat who works for Democratic causes and candidates. Our party has a better vision for the country than the regression, corporatism, corruption, incivility, and oligarchy that Trump and the Republican Party offer.

Anyone still unsure about what Democrats stand for, please re-read the first few paragraphs of this column. Our views don't fit on a hat. But they do fit in an open mind.

What is "White Culture"?

September 2017

I'm white. A white supremacist would offer me a year's pay for my Ancestry DNA results. I'm so white that I'm almost translucent. White people give directions by pointing at me on the street and saying, "Over there, by the white guy."

So you'd think I'd know what "white culture" is. Not so. The people ranting that they're victims of attacks on "white culture" never seem to define the term adequately.

"White culture" often gets reworked as "white heritage" and "white history." Look closely enough at anyone who uses these terms, and you're likely to find "white supremacist" just beneath the surface. These are the folks who recently rebranded themselves as the "alt-right." They say that statues erected to reinforce Jim Crow are somehow sacred. They spread the nonsense that the Confederate flag isn't about slavery.

Donald Trump himself recently said that moving Confederate statues from public grounds is, "trying to take away our culture ... our history." He left out the word "white," but otherwise sounded just like the Charlottesville white supremacists.

Does the Confederacy represent the best that white people have accomplished in human history? I hope not. Believing your race has the divine right to own people of a different race should inspire shame, not pride. For people who feel a strange need to boast about Caucasian accomplishments, classical music and Renaissance art are much better. Ice hockey and pizza are far superior to slavery. Basically, anything white people have ever done beats slavery. Yet white supremacists cling to slavery and riot to defend Confederate statues.

"White heritage" and "white history" are often just more socially acceptable versions of the term "white pride." Mentally healthy people are proud of their family, their career, how they work toward making the world a better place, and how they've overcome obstacles to succeed.

"Black pride" isn't simply the inverse of "white pride," but a reference to overcoming the obstacles of institutional racism. "White pride," by contrast, celebrates institutional racism. "White pride" is really about "white power." White supremacists aren't afraid of losing their "culture." They're afraid of losing their white monopoly.

Life must be very sad for those who measure the accident of their skin color as their greatest source of pride. Unfortunately, these folks consider their whiteness no accident. They believe being white is a sign from God of their superiority. That's called, "white delusion." White supremacists are generally the least "supreme" white people around.

Hillary Clinton had these white supremacists in mind when she described some Trump supporters as "deplorables." Her candor might not have been politically expedient, but the substance of her claim is accurate: Not all Trump supporters are racists, but the vast majority of racists are Trump supporters.

For example, no one was surprised when the official newspaper of the KKK endorsed Trump for president. Well, many were surprised that KKK members could actually read. How do Americans who voted for Trump feel about the fact that they sided with the KKK in the presidential election? Any regrets?

Let's play "Who said it?" Who has repeatedly called himself a "gene believer"? Who said, "I'm proud of my German blood. There's no question about it. Great stuff." Was that Trump or David Duke, former KKK leader, Charlottesville white supremacist agitator, and vocal Trump supporter?

Those are Trump quotes, of course. (Look 'em up.) Sure, Duke has said worse, but he's a pretty low bar for comparison. We can't ignore the fact that Trump mimics white supremacist rhetoric. During the recent statue debate, Trump even compared our nation's founders to the Confederate traitors who fought to preserve slavery: "I wonder, is it George Washington next week? And is it Thomas Jefferson the week after?"

That's the verbatim argument that white supremacists use to justify their rage over moving Confederate statues. Duke himself beamed with pride, tweeting, "Thank you President Trump for your honesty and courage." For some Trump supporters, smearing our founders represents "honesty and courage." Deplorable, indeed.

Trump's racial rhetoric trickles down and emboldens closet racists to vent terrible views. In a recent Facebook discussion, I observed a white guy repeatedly telling a black woman to "get over" slavery because she was "never a slave herself." That may be the worst example of "whitesplaining" I've ever encountered.

I would hope we could all agree that white people shouldn't dictate how black people should feel about slavery. A better starting point would be empathy for people different from ourselves so that we could learn from each other instead of forcing limited views on an issue as complex as America's racial history.

Trump hasn't shown an aptitude for complexity. Instead, he cultivated bigotry by blaming "many sides" for the racist violence in Charlottesville. Then he pardoned Joe Arpiao and ended DACA protections—indefensible actions that serve no purpose other than exciting his worst supporters. Polls show a large majority of Americans oppose these moves, but you can bet that at least 90% of white supremacists agree with Trump on Arpaio and DACA.

Republican politicians have courted the racist voting block for half a century, and now Trump gives racists a presidential champion. Future historians will not look kindly on Trump and his enablers during a time when our first African-American president has been followed by the KKK-endorsed president. If that's what passes for "white culture" during the Trump era, then it's hard to imagine a more disappointing quantum leap backward.

We Deserve Better than Trump

October 2017

Early in the semester during a community college public speaking class can be an anxiety-filled time for most of the students I've seen over my decades of teaching. But Allie seemed especially distracted recently as she discussed her upcoming speech—something about a wedding and complicated travel plans. Then Allie's cell phone rang. She gasped, excused herself, and rushed from the room, phone cradled to her heart.

She soon returned, looking stunned. She collapsed into her seat and revealed that the caller was her mother in Puerto Rico. Allie hadn't heard from her since Hurricane Maria hit the island the previous week and didn't even know if she was alive until that moment.

The wedding Allie had mentioned was her own, scheduled for the following week, and the travel difficulties involved her mother's attendance. The hurricane had disrupted carefully crafted plans and left her family frantic.

As Allie told us that her mother was about to board a flight and would the at the wedding, she broke into relieved sobs. Her classmates comforted her with hugs and kind words. For a moment, we forgot about the upcoming speeches and our superficial differences. No one was divided by race, ethnicity, gender, age, beliefs, or orientation. Our empathy for Allie's barely averted family tragedy and her upcoming wedding connected us through our common humanity.

Driving home that night with Allie's story still fresh in my mind, I listened to two audiobooks. One was "Devil's Bargain," Joshua Green's account of two mean-spirited con artists (Steve Bannon and Donald Trump) who stoked fear and anger just enough to make Trump our terrible president.

That terrible president has botched the response to Hurricane Maria. Republicans and hurricanes generally don't mix. Remember Bush and Katrina? Republicans think government is incompetent, so poor disaster response isn't a bug in the Republican operating system. It's a feature.

Trump couples general Republican incompetence with inhumanity. While Puerto Rico suffered, he attacked football players exercising their constitutional right to protest against violence. His venomous comments were harsher than any he's ever directed toward white supremacists or murderous dictators.

The second audiobook was Hillary Clinton's election memoir, "What Happened." Clinton's book is a healing balm for the injuries of Trump's presidency. She recalls the election with justified anger and frustration, but she ultimately returns to her campaign motto, "Stronger Together," as a way to resist Trump's agenda. Clinton, unlike Trump, views government as "we the people," a nation united by common bonds, not divided by fear of diversity.

How would Clinton handle Hurricane Maria? Much like President Obama handled Hurricane Sandy in 2012, with competence and empathy. Democrats believe government serves the people, especially our most vulnerable citizens in times of need. Democrats in Congress don't vote against disaster funding outside their home states and then beg for similar relief when their constituents get hit. Republicans do so routinely.

Clinton recommended sending the navy hospital ship Comfort to Puerto Rico immediately after the hurricane. Her call to action led to more than a quarter of a million signatures of support at Change.org. The Trump administration delayed but eventually did approve plans to send the Comfort.

Meanwhile, Trump repeatedly embarrassed himself. He childishly claimed that helping Puerto Rico was hard because it's "in the middle of an ocean ... a big ocean." He criticized Puerto Rico's "massive debt" and "broken infrastructure," referred to San Juan's mayor as "nasty" (his favorite insult for women who stand up to his bullying), and tweeted that Puerto Ricans are "ingrates" who "want everything to be done for them."

Then, typically, Trump retreated to one of his golf clubs. With astonishing tone deafness, he dedicated a meaningless golf trophy to the hurricane victims. Unlike Texas and Florida, which got tepidly better responses to recent hurricanes, Puerto Rico has no electoral votes for president, so Trump sees nothing to gain from actually helping the citizens there.

Things got even worse when Trump's traveling circus visited Puerto Rico. He claimed that the disaster was "throwing our budget out of whack" and downplayed the death toll. Then (not kidding) he tossed (for real) rolls of paper towels (Google it if you don't believe me) to a group of hurricane survivors (like a rotund emperor tossing scraps to hungry peasants).

If Clinton (or any Democrat) were president, she wouldn't insult American citizens as they struggled. Nor would she scapegoat professional athletes protesting to make our nation safer.

Clinton's motto, "Stronger Together," is also a good description of my classes. Just as Clinton appealed to the intelligence and aspirations of voters, I set high academic standards, and Allie and her classmates know that they can all work together to realize their potential. Creating a learning community nurtures growth, so everyone does better.

How would Trump teach a diverse community college class? He'd pit students against each other while his underlings did the real work. By semester's end, he'd insult, degrade, and expel everyone except his anointed favorite. Learning, growth, and community wouldn't stand a chance. Sadly, his presidency hasn't been much different.

The United States deserves better. Allie and her classmates and her mother deserve better. Even the voters that Trump hoodwinked deserve better. We all do. We've had better presidents in recent years. The 2016 popular vote indicates that we want a better president, and I'm hopeful that we'll have a better president again soon.

Yes, of Course, Better Gun-Safety Laws Would Help

November 2017

Republicans follow the same script after every mass shooting. "Too soon. Disrespectful to talk about laws, unless it supports our pro-gun agenda. Thoughts and prayers. Buh-bye!" This script has become a pathetic and predictable reflex that our nation needs to reject

Donald Trump has made the Republican script even worse. "It's a little bit soon to go into it," he said when asked about gun laws after the recent Texas church shooting. Then he did "go into it," inaccurately claiming that better gun laws would have led to "hundreds more dead" by preventing the church neighbor from shooting at the killer.

Trump's supporters immediately parroted his obvious lie, even though it's clear that stronger background check enforcement would have prevented the killer from legally getting weapons but would not have affected the law-abiding citizen who confronted the killer.

Trump also said, "mental health is the problem here," which is ironic coming from someone who signed a Republican-backed bill making it easier for people with serious mental illness to get guns. The irony is deepened by the fact that Trump and Republicans in Congress have been working to destroy Obamacare, which includes the most significant expansion of mental health care access in American history.

When Republicans actually do discuss gun laws, they almost always put forth the view that nothing can be done. Following the Las Vegas shooting, the Gazette's regular conservative columnist devoted one thousand words to come to the hopeless, helpless, hapless conclusion that changes to gun laws aren't "solutions" but merely "tokens."

One Trump-supporting friend of mine put that viewpoint more concisely in a Facebook post after the Las Vegas shooting: "Changing gun laws won't help. Criminals will be criminals and that's that."

That view isn't just a fatalistic surrender—it's factually wrong. Improving gun-safety laws can help.

Obviously, no law prevents every crime. But laws do reduce crime. No one with any sense would say that we shouldn't have laws against child molestation or burglary because those child molesters and burglars would find a way to molest and burgle anyway.

Can you imagine a Republican saying we shouldn't have laws against terrorism after a terrorist attack? Trump didn't come on national television after the New York City attack and shrug his shoulders and say, "Laws against terrorism are tokens but not solutions. Terrorists will be terrorists and that's that. Wadda ya gonna do?"

Gun laws are no different. Better laws that make it harder for dangerous people to get dangerous weapons would make mass shootings less likely.

The recent Las Vegas and Texas shootings are instructive examples. Here are some concrete ways that improved gun-safety laws that might have stopped those terrible tragedies:

1) If we still had the assault weapons ban that Republicans let expire, then the shooters would have had a harder time getting their semi-automatic rifles.

2) If high-capacity magazines were banned, then the shooters would have had a harder time firing so many shots at one time, killing so many people.

3) If bump stocks were banned, then the Las Vegas shooter would have had a harder time converting his semi-automatics to fire like automatics, killing so many people.

4) If Nevada didn't have such loose laws about carrying weapons, then the shooter might have drawn more attention transporting multiple rifles to his hotel room, possibly raising alarms that might have led to preventing the shooting altogether.

5) If Nevada didn't have such loose laws regulating their frequent gun shows, then the shooter might not have blended so easily into the gun culture of Las Vegas, possibly raising alarms that might have prevented the shooting altogether.

6) If we had better background checks that flagged someone purchasing massive stockpiles of weapons and ammunition, then the Las Vegas shooter would have had a harder time getting so many guns and killing so many people.

7) If we had better health coverage and better background checks to identify mental health and domestic violence issues, then the shooters would have had a harder time getting guns to commit their crimes.

These changes to the laws aren't perfect, but they're an improvement Any one of them might have stopped the Las Vegas and Texas shooters from being able to kill and injure so many people. Obviously, current gun laws didn't stop them.

None of these improvements to gun laws would stop law-abiding people from owning a reasonable number of reasonable guns for protection. But improvements to the current laws could reduce gun crimes, especially the mass shootings that tear apart the fabric of our nation as surely as they tear apart the bodies of the innocent victims.

Republicans are fond of sending "thoughts and prayers" after every incident of horrible gun violence. I send my love and empathy to the victims of all mass shootings, along with my thoughts and prayers.

For my thoughts, I'm thinking that Republicans in Congress need to stop bowing down to the death-profiteering gun lobby and pass some meaningful improvements to laws that could help reduce gun violence.

For my prayers, I'm praying that Americans will have the good sense to vote out the Republicans who care more about gun lobby endorsements than they do about the lives of the American people.

Alabama Election Will Reveal GOP Heart and Mind

December 2017

Time Magazine just named "The Silence Breakers" as its Person(s) of the Year. I respect, admire, and empathize with these courageous survivors who have revealed their sexual abuse at the hands of men in positions of power. They've spoken out despite often being disbelieved, ridiculed, and threatened.

I confess that I've previously admired a few of the accused men (chiefly Al Franken). Almost all have apologized and faced the consequences. That doesn't absolve them, but it's a start. Others, I've detested. They've denied everything despite mountains of evidence against them. Republican Senate candidate Roy Moore and Republican President Donald Trump are two such detestable deniers.

Moore was a terrible candidate even before he was accused of inappropriate sexual conduct with many young women and girls, ranging from aggressively pursuing "dates" with teenagers while in his thirties, to forced physical contact and kissing, to clear sexual assault of a fourteen-year-old girl.

In normal times, these well-researched, credible accusations would be more than enough to force a candidate to withdraw. But these are not normal times. In Moore's Alabama, too many people follow a confused, right-wing, patriarchal version of Christian Sharia mixed with hatred of basic journalism bolstered by Trump's dishonest cries of "fake news."

Moore's opponent, Democrat Doug Jones, has a different history with young girls. As a prosecutor in the late 1990s, he convicted two KKK members who murdered four children in a 1963 Birmingham church bombing. As of this writing, Moore is ahead in most polls approaching the December 12 election. Alabamans may just choose a Republican child abuser over a Democrat who jailed racist child murderers. Let that sink in.

Trump has now fully endorsed Moore's Senate run. Like Moore, Trump has been accused multiple times. More than a dozen women have claimed that Trump grabbed, fondled, or kiss them without consent in a clear pattern of abusive behavior spanning decades.

Trump has even been accused of rape, once by his first wife Ivana in 1989 and once by a woman who claimed that Trump raped her at a party in 1994 when she was thirteen and threatened to murder her and her family if she told anyone. Ivana eventually backtracked to say that Trump hadn't raped her "in a literal or criminal sense," whatever that means. The other accuser dropped her lawsuit against Trump just before the 2016 election because she received "numerous threats."

Major media outlets have yet to question Trump about these incredibly disturbing rape accusations. It's hard to imagine any other public figure being given a free pass in similar circumstances. So much for the "liberal media" that Trump loathes.

Trump has, of course, been recorded bragging about his abusive exploits. In the infamous "Access Hollywood" tape, Trump speaks coarsely about "moving on" a married woman not long after his own wedding to current wife Melania. Revealing that this married woman rebuffed his advances, Trump then ridiculed her appearance, probably to assuage his wounded ego.

He then admitted to being "automatically attracted" and powerless to resist attractive women, even popping mints in case "I start kissing" Arianne Zucker, the woman waiting to lead him through a television set. He described Zucker by saying, "Oh, it looks good," referring to her with a pronoun that normal people use for an object rather than a human being.

And, of course, Trump uttered the words that should have ended his political career: "I just start kissing them. It's like a magnet. Just kiss. I don't even wait. And when you're a star, they let you do it. You can do anything. Grab 'em by the p***y."

It's astonishing that anyone could have voted for Trump after hearing him make these nauseating comments. To clear up any confusion, grabbing someone's genitals without consent is sexual assault. For anyone who thinks it isn't, try having a big, sweaty, aggressive jerk like Trump grab your crotch without your consent. Good luck not feeling assaulted.

Trump half-heartedly "apologized" when the tape was released. Then he tried to explain it away as "locker room talk," claiming that Bill Clinton had said and done far worse. Recent reports have noted that Trump claims the "Access Hollywood" tape is a fake—despite his previous admission and rationalizations. Billy Bush, the television host who shared this disgusting conversation with Trump, recently called out Trump's delusion: "Of course he said it."

In a previous act of delusion, Trump said before the election, "All of these liars [his accusers] will be sued after the election is over." More than a year later, he hasn't sued anyone. If he did, he'd have to testify under oath about his actions. He'd sooner drink bleach than be compelled by law to tell the truth.

Bill Clinton testified under oath about his sexual behavior, and he faced impeachment over his misguided attempt to downplay his affair with Monica Lewinski. What would happen if Trump testified under oath about his multiple instances of sexual misconduct? He'd lie, of course. His lies would make Clinton's seem like a speck of dust compared to Trump's dumpster of dishonesty. Would the Republican-controlled Congress have the courage to impeach him for his lies? That's unlikely.

Moore's candidacy portends how sexual abuse will be handled moving forward. Will Republicans refuse consequences for their politicians' crimes, as they have with Trump? Or will they inch toward calling these men to account, as Democrats have done? Will we fall into the predator-enabling past or progress toward a future where women are treated as fully equal human beings?

One thing is certain: We'll know the heart and mind of the Republican Party after Tuesday's election in Alabama.

"Make America Great Again"
Needs a Few Disclaimers

January 2018

I'm typing these words on the morning of New Year's Eve, 2017. Each sentence is punctuated by a coughing fit. Once again, my wife Betsy and I have found ourselves sick during the holiday season, something that has become a pattern in recent years.

The over-the-counter medication we're taking claims in big type on the front of the box to relieve "headache, fever, sore throat, minor aches and pains, sneezing, runny nose, and cough." Spoiler alert: It doesn't.

A quick glance at the back of the medication box reveals in much smaller type—the "fine print," as it's called—some potential side effects: severe liver damage, skin reddening, blisters, and rash. No thank you, please. Further fine-print shows that these pills can cause excitability and drowsiness. Really? Simultaneously? That could make for a fun New Year's Eve if we weren't so sick.

We've all seen television ads for the promise of various medications: An unfortunate woman/man/child mopes across the cloudy scene, unable to keep up with happy grandchildren/children/friends. The downcast narrator blames everything on some heretofore untreatable and incurable ailment.

Suddenly, the sun breaks through, and our protagonist launches from the bed/couch/bench to stride/run/leap into happy activities—all thanks to the latest miracle drug. "Ask your doctor if 'Yanoslivator' is right for you!" the newly joyful narrator crows, knowing that, of course, Yanoslivator is right for you if its marked-up price is covered by your insurance plan.

The next two minutes of the television ad shows the delightful frolicking brought about by Yanoslivator. Meanwhile, however, the narrator dismissively tosses out a lengthy list of Yanoslivator's side effects, disclaimers, and cautions. "Yanoslivator has caused suicide in laboratory animals. Don't take Yanoslivator if you breathe air. In rare cases, Yanoslivator will make you chew off your left hand."

Is all of that Yanoslivator-induced frolicking worth it if you've eaten your left hand? That's up to your insurance carrier.

Donald Trump is the Yanoslivator of politics. His re-election campaign commercials could begin with images of what Trump himself has called "American carnage," the terrible state of the nation before he took office. Remember the horrors when our previous president spoke in complete sentences, when the Supreme Court ruled we all had equal protection of the laws, when Neo-Nazis were embarrassed to march in public?

How could we ever frolic again after such carnage?

Then Trump could stride onto our television screen in his lumpy suit and extra-long necktie. Hallelujah! We've all been cured by just one dose of Trump's Make America Great Again (MAGA, for short)! The wealthy and corporations have been relieved of their odious tax burdens! "America-firsters" no longer have to pretend to like our international allies! We are finally allowed to say "Merry Christmas" again without being instantly drone-bombed by a Muslim president! What sensible American wouldn't want more of Trump's delicious snake oil?

As the television ad continues, Trump could lurch from podium to podium, gesticulating with his digitally enlarged hands, as a small voice lists just a few of the side-effects, disclaimers, cautions associated with following this incompetent narcissist who would sell all our souls for another five minutes of power:

"MAGA is not valid in the United States of America. For propaganda purposes only. Not intended as a factual statement. Side effects include intense regret, embarrassment, loss of health insurance, and increased threat from climate change. Activation requires profound ignorance and intolerant world view and working knowledge of Russian language. Actual benefits limited to corporations and the wealthy. Tiki-torches sold separately."

I may have been naïve enough to think that I wouldn't get sick this year between Christmas and the New Year. And I was optimistic enough to think that some weak, over-the-counter pills might relieve my sleepless nights, hacking cough, and hours spent shoveling snow while nursing atomic body aches in every muscle and bone.

But I wasn't confused enough to ignore Trump's obvious side effects—not in 2016, not in 2017, and certainly not as we move into 2018.

Actor and comedian Steve Martin once penned a marvelous short story titled, "Side Effects." The story begins thusly: "Dosage: Take two tablets every six hours for joint pain. Side Effects: This drug may cause joint pain." There's not a more appropriate passage in all of American literature to sum up the reign of Trump.

In 2016, some Americans looked at our nation and said, "Hey, let's elect this Trump guy! He'll fix everything!" It's like they had the sniffles and said, "Hey, let's chug antifreeze! That'll fix everything!"

Even worse, some Americans are now praising the curative qualities of antifreeze, claiming that Trump has "drained the swamp" even though he's installed himself as the King of the Swamp. They're claiming that Trump is "making America great again" even though they have no clue what makes America great in the first place.

As the new year dawns, let's remember that Trump will continue to sicken our country in 2018. The upcoming midterm elections can't cure everything, but they're as close to an effective treatment as we have available. If we don't resist Trump's attacks on our nation, and we don't campaign and vote in the mid-term elections, then our side effects will surely include a lingering taste of antifreeze.

Is Trump a Good Role Model?

February 2018

Who comes to mind when we think about role models? Parents, teachers, coaches, bosses, police officers, firefighters, soldiers, doctors, nurses—even celebrities and sports stars can serve as role models. Unfortunately, we all know stories of how these traditional role models also provide negative examples. Sometimes it's hard to tell who we can trust to guide future generations.

What about politicians?

Our "public servants" should inspire us. Some do. Barack Obama remains a voice of reason, pillar of personal integrity, and an exemplary husband and father. Senator Tammy Duckworth is a true hero who lost her legs in the Iraq War, and now she continues to serve in Congress while pregnant with her second child just weeks before turning fifty. Here at home, Representative Jim McGovern inspires with his passion, energy, and humor despite our difficult political times.

Unfortunately, most politicians aren't highly regarded as role models. For every Obama, Duckworth, and McGovern, we can all name plenty more who betray the public trust. Some behave so egregiously in and out of office that the public roundly condemns them. Yet some of the worst get an inexplicable "mulligan" for their bad acts.

Case in point: A recent Quinnipiac University poll revealed that 72% of Republicans believe Donald Trump is a good role model for kids. That's deeply disturbing. I didn't think 72 individual human beings would consider Trump a good role model, let alone millions of Republicans.

Fortunately, the poll indicates sanity outside the Republican Party: 99% of Democrats and 71% of Independents said that Trump isn't a good role model. So what happened to the GOP?

Republicans used to be the anti-Hollywood party but now swoon for a reality TV host. They used to be the "bootstraps" party but now revere someone born with a full set of golden cutlery. They used to tout law-and-order but are now accomplices to a con artist openly trying to undermine the law-enforcement professionals investigating him for collusion and obstruction of justice. They used to preach "family values" but now embrace a philandering harasser.

Republicans praise Trump's alleged leadership skills, but he can't even avoid a government shutdown with his own party controlling Congress. They parrot Trump's pseudo-patriotic nationalism while ignoring how he twitches to Putin's puppet strings. They call Trump the ultimate winner even though he lost the popular vote by millions.

Meanwhile, Trump bears no resemblance to true role models.

Who would hire Trump as a grade-school teacher? Linguists have analyzed his speeches and found fourth-grade-level language development, but speaking down to children (or adults) isn't a virtue. And Trump's self-confessed aversion to reading wouldn't make him much of a role model for doing homework.

Who would trust Trump to chaperone a prom? He has frequently spoken in sexualized terms about young women (including his own daughter). He entered the dressing room for Miss Teen USA contestants while girls as young as fifteen were changing clothes. And he has said of girls as young as ten that he'd be dating them in a few years.

Who would want Trump to speak at a Boy Scout meeting? Oh, wait. Someone did. At the 2017 Boy Scout Jamboree, Trump ignored the organizers' instructions not to politicize his comments as he bragged about his election win, criticized Obama, swore, and referenced "the hottest people" at a cocktail party he attended. The head of the Boy Scouts had to issue an apology for the president's behavior a few days later.

Who would send a young person considering military enlistment to Trump? Trump weaseled five deferments for heel spurs to avoid service in Vietnam—although he continued to play sports at the time. He has called his youthful exploits with multiple sex partners, "my personal Vietnam" that made him a "brave soldier." When recently asked which heel had the spur, Trump couldn't remember.

Who would tell a friend to ask Trump for marital advice? Well, can you say "porn star"? How about "p*ssy grabber"? Do Republicans know that the p*ssy grabber and porn star incidents happened shortly before and shortly after Trump's current wife Melania gave birth to their child? Enough said on that subject.

Who would recommend that kids follow Trump on social media? His infamous Twitter feed is like a handbook for cyberbullying, complete with threats, mindless insults, and re-tweets of hate groups and white supremacists. Perhaps Melania's invisible anti-bullying initiative is just brilliant trolling to embarrass her horrible husband.

Who would extol Trump as a "cannot tell a lie" example of presidential honesty? His whole campaign was based on the lie that he's qualified for office. He rose to political prominence behind the racist "birther" lie about Obama and has since told thousands of documented falsehoods. He lies equally about inconsequential trifles and life-and-death issues. During his recent State of the Union address, the fact-checking website PolitiFact.com literally crashed as millions of people monitored his dishonesty.

Who would want Trump as a boss? Most people don't enjoy working for someone who outsources production to other countries, has multiple business bankruptcies, stiffs his employees and contractors, was fined for discriminatory business practices, and has been sued thousands of times. His television signature was arrogantly grunting, "you're fired!" Trump may fancy himself "America's CEO," but he's the textbook definition of a toxic boss.

Overall, anyone who thinks Trump is a positive role model has clearly lost touch with reality. Only Republicans still fawn over Trump. The rest of us are looking toward a real role model, Robert Mueller, to cancel this failing reality show.

Trump's School Shooting Boast is Terrible Advice

March 2018

Donald Trump's proposal to arm teachers is being widely and rightly criticized by law-enforcement experts and education professionals. As a teacher myself, I understand how bringing weapons into the classroom changes teaching and learning from a nurturing activity that makes the world a better place into a militarized atmosphere where violence is more likely and more deadly.

When I look around at my colleagues during faculty meetings, I'm thankful that I don't see people with cowboy/Rambo fantasies. I'm sure they feel the same way about me. We already have full-time jobs as teachers. Being armed security guards is another career altogether. And any teacher who longs to strap on a sidearm as they interact with students on a daily basis has no business in any classroom.

But pushing to arm teachers isn't the worst thing Trump has said recently, as difficult as that is to believe. He attacked members of the Parkland, Florida, sheriff's department for not rushing into Marjory Stoneman Douglas High School as a deadly shooting took place there last month. "They weren't exactly Medal of Honor winners, all right?" Trump opined. "The way they performed was frankly disgusting."

Then Trump degraded the standards for presidential discourse to perhaps the most absurd level ever: "I really believe I'd run in there even if I didn't have a weapon."

Setting aside his attack on law enforcement officers before all the facts of the situation have been uncovered, Trump simply sounds delusional. His credibility as a man of heroic action is questionable at best. Many observers have rightly pointed out that Trump avoided service in Vietnam on tenuous medical grounds, earning him the nickname, "Cadet Bone Spurs." The words, "frankly disgusting," best describe Trump's own well-documented misbehavior, often a mix of rampant hedonism and self-aggrandizement unbefitting an actual hero.

But Trump's false bravado shows something even worse than his gross personal failing. His assertion that he would have rushed into the school is exactly what law enforcement experts advise people not—repeat, *not*—to do in an active-shooter situation.

Moving toward a shooting puts a person in greater danger, obviously. More importantly, such rash action complicates the situation for law-enforcement officers. They don't know whether a random person rushing into a crime scene is the shooter or a frantic bystander. There's a good chance that officers would be forced to fire on someone following Trump's fantasy example.

Assuming officers determine that a particular intruder isn't a shooter, they then have to divert their attention and resources to keep this person safe instead of pursuing the actual shooter. That diversion gives the shooter more time to escape or even kill more people. Basically, the misguided, pseudo-heroic charge that Trump described is much more likely to make the situation far worse, not better.

The best strategy recommended by experts during a shooting is called, "Run-Hide-Fight." Option one: Run to safety away from the shooting. Option two: Hide in a secure area out of the shooter's view and try to fortify your position. Option Three: If running and/or hiding are impossible, as a last resort, try to incapacitate the shooter any way you can.

The Parkland sheriff's deputies may not have acted as heroically as possible, but we don't have all the facts yet, and neither does Trump. We may never know exactly what happened. Now is not the time to blame police officers with a scarcity of evidence. None of us, armed or unarmed, know how we would react to an adversary with a semiautomatic rifle. I hope no one reading these words ever has to find out.

Whatever the officers' behavior might have been, that doesn't change the fact that "Run-Hide-Fight" are the best options. Of course, these "best" options are all terrible because they constitute damage control instead of prevention. The actual best option is the one Republican politicians have opposed for decades: enacting sensible gun-safety laws that help keep dangerous weapons out of the hands of dangerous people.

As Trump, his fellow Republicans, and the NRA push to arm teachers, their motives are transparent. They know that providing guns, ammunition, and training for even a modest percentage of teachers would be a weapons windfall for the gun industry that would easily soar into millions if not billions of dollars. Just as what

President Eisenhower called the "Military-Industrial Complex" profits from continuous war, the "Gun-Fear Complex" would profit from militarizing our schools.

The "Run-Hide-Fight" video produced by the Department of Homeland Security is easy to find with a simple internet search. The video dramatizes a mass shooting, which can be disturbing to watch. But it could also save the lives of people who might find themselves in such a horrible situation. I wish Trump would watch and learn.

This video reminds us that, as in all things, we should seek the guidance of professionals who know what they're talking about while we tune out the Misinformer-in-Chief. Not only does Trump's boast that he would rush into an active shooting sound like the ranting of a bloviating narcissist, but he's also offering dreadful advice that puts people's lives in danger. His comments, like most of his presidency, are a menace to the nation.

"March For Our Lives" Illustrates Divided Nation

April 2018

Our nation has been divided along various fault lines since our founding. The latest division pits teenagers who don't want to get shot against conservatives who seem upset that these teenagers are speaking out about not wanting to get shot.

That seems absurd, but that's the country we inhabit these days. Many students who survived the Parkland shooting are calling for common-sense gun-safety laws that could reduce the likelihood and severity of mass shootings. They've been articulate and passionate voices since their lives were interrupted by gunfire that killed many of their friends.

In March, they led the March for Our Lives, one of the largest demonstrations in American history. The main march swelled the streets of Washington, DC, while millions more marched in cities across the globe. I joined thousands of other marchers here in Northampton that day.

Our current national divide can be seen in the contrast between the signs carried by young people at the Northampton march and the comments from conservative "adults" on television and in social media.

Here's a sign I saw held by a student at the Northampton march: "Save Kids Not Guns." Sounds good to me.

Here's a right-wing attack against the students: Republican U.S. Representative Steve King mocked student activist Emma Gonzales in a Facebook post because she wore a Cuban flag patch on her jacket, somehow implying that her heritage disqualified her from advocating on the issue of guns. When called out on the bigoted post, King claimed that only a "brainwashed lefty" would object to his views.

Here's another student sign: "One Child Is Worth More Than All The Guns On Earth."

Here's another right wing-attack: Many conservative blogs spread the false accusation that student activist David Hogg wasn't even in school during the shooting. Their claim was quickly debunked, but the attackers' critical thinking skills disintegrated the moment they thought they could discredit Hogg. They ended up discrediting themselves.

Another sign: "I Want To Live To See Graduation."

Another right-wing attack: Fox News contributor Thomi Lahren tweeted that, "Simply being anti-NRA is not a solution. March FOR something, not just against everything." Lahren was so blinded by her pro-gun agenda that she was unable to read the word "for" in the name "March 'for' our lives."

Another sign: "History Has Its Eyes On You."

Another attack: Fox News host Laura Ingraham accused Hogg of "whining" about not being accepted by some colleges. When advertisers left her show in droves after her insensitive and nonsensical comment, she backtracked "in the spirit of Holy Week." It's a shame that Ingraham needed the Easter holiday and sponsor boycott to inspire her to show basic human decency toward a mass shooting survivor.

Sign: "Policy Change Not Thoughts and Prayers."

Attack: Former Republican Senator Rick Santorum said, "How about kids—instead of looking to someone else to solve their problem—do something about maybe taking CPR classes or trying to deal with situations that, when there is a violent shooter, that you can actually respond to that?" It's bad enough that Santorum thinks CPR is an appropriate treatment for gunshot wounds. It's worse that his statement implies that school shootings are inevitable. But the worst part is that Santorum, a former lawmaker, thinks advocating for better laws is "looking to someone else to solve your problem." No wonder he's a "former" senator.

Sign: "I Want to Read Books Not Eulogies."

Attack: One right-wing social media meme showed an altered photo of Gonzales ripping the Constitution in half. In reality, she ripped a shooting target in half. Another meme showed a shaven-headed young woman swinging an umbrella at a truck. The caption claimed Gonzales was "attacking a Second Amendment supporter's truck." This was actually a decade-old photo of Britney Spears. Oops, they did it again—lying that is.

Sign: "Fear Has No Place in Schools."

Attack: An aid to a Florida state representative claimed that Gonzales and Hogg were "crisis actors" who pretended to be part of the tragedy. A Republican candidate for Maine State Senate called Gonzales a "skin head lesbian" and "moron moonbat." He also called Hogg a "moron" and a "baldfaced liar." An aid to a New York State Senator posted a photo of Hogg with his arm raised alongside a photo of Hitler giving a Nazi salute. Classy, these Republicans are not.

Sign: "I Want To Live To See Graduation."

Attack: Washed-up musician Ted Nugent made perhaps the most ludicrous attack on the students, calling them "ignorant and dangerously stupid" and claiming that "They have no soul." Nugent isn't an expert on having a soul. Among a long list of hateful statements, he once yelled, "Obama, he's a piece of sh*t. I told him to suck on my machine gun. Hey, Hillary, you might want to ride one of these into the sunset, you worthless b*tch," while holding assault rifles aloft at a concert. Despite such disgusting public comments, Nugent remains a frequent contributor to right-wing media, a board member of the NRA, and a recent guest of Donald Trump at the White House.

Finally, here's a sign held by one of the many adults who came out to support the young activists at the Northampton march: "We'll Follow Our Students All The Way To The Ballot Box."

Our nation faces a choice. Do we support young people who don't want to die in a mass shooting, or do we support people who seem to have guns where their souls should be? A good place to make that choice is in the voting booth at the upcoming midterm election.

Critical Thinking is the Cure for Fake News

May 2018

Donald Trump and his supporters are currently the leading purveyors of "alternative facts" and "fake news," but they didn't invent these phenomena. They simply took advantage of a political climate that discouraged critical thinking and promoted sloppy and inaccurate analysis of important issues.

Case in point: For years, my Republican friends have sent me what they call a "news report" claiming that a college professor had a class full of naïve students who were big fans of "Obama's Socialism."

The professor told the class, "Let's test Obama's plan." Everyone's grade would be averaged, and all students would receive the same course grade at the end of the semester, just like "Obama's Socialism."

To make a long story short, the students all got progressively lazier and failed the course. The moral to the story is supposed to be that Socialism rewards "takers" more than "makers," so Socialism will never work as well as Capitalism.

The friends who send me this story always want to know what I think of it because they assume that, as a liberal college professor who voted for Obama, I must be a Socialist.

My response is two words that can't be printed in this newspaper: the first refers to an intact adult male bovine, the second an indecorous word for excrement. Then I apply two more socially acceptable words to their fanciful tale: critical thinking.

First, no reputable college would tolerate that kind of grading system. Any professor who averages student grades is guilty of professional misconduct. The students aren't mad at Socialism. They're mad at instructor malfeasance. Fact-checkers have pointed out that this supposed "news story" isn't based on real events, obviously, but is just another made-up raindrop in the monsoon of right-wing fake news.

Second, classes aren't economies. Grades aren't money. The analogy is superficial and strained at best.

76

Third, as most fact-checkers have also noted, the fake grade system sounds more like Communism than Socialism, although that's not even a good analogy.

Fourth, the concept of "Obama's Socialism" is another complete fiction. "Obama's Socialism" is a made-up, scare-tactic term originated by Republican spin-doctors to scare people away from any government program that actually helps everyday Americans instead of just corporations and the wealthy.

Just for fun, I've recently started providing my conservative friends with a different fictional scenario that I made up myself, unlike the one they parroted from their fake news sources.

At the beginning of the semester, the students told the professor that they were all fans of "Trump's Capitalism." The professor responded by proposing a class experiment to test "Trump's Capitalism." He told the students to put all the cash they had with them into an envelope with their name on it.

"Pass those envelopes up to me," our fictional professor said. "The students who submit the most money will start out with an A in the class. The second tier with start with a B, the next tier a C, and so on." With a sad face, the professor concluded, "If your envelope is empty, well, then you unfortunate souls will begin the class with an F. But you can pull yourself up by your bootstraps to improve your original grade. Of course, if you're happy with your initial grade, you don't have to do anything."

"Wait, that's not fair," some students objected, particularly those whose envelops were light on cash. "Stop complaining and start studying!" the students with fat envelops called out.

For the first few weeks of the semester, the wealthy students spent class time surfing social media, while the poorer ones took meticulous notes and asked well-considered questions. Eventually, only the poorest students continued coming to class, studying, and doing homework, while the wealthy ones played video games on their dorm room couches all day, content with their grades.

At the end of the semester, the wealthy students all earned top grades, while the poor ones struggled to pass even with strong work on their exams and assignments. And some failed outright because they were stuck in such a deep hole from the start. When they complained, the professor just said, "Hey, that's exactly how Trump's Capitalism works. Are you still big fans?"

My friends are outraged: "Come on! That's a slanted interpretation of Capitalism! It's not really like that!"

That's the point, of course. My story is an obvious exaggeration of some very real problems that can surface when Capitalism is abused. The folks who bemoan my story should at least apply the same minimum of critical thinking to the absurd "Obama's Socialism" story as well. But they don't.

Unfortunately, Trump himself accepts as fact the fake reporting of alt-right Brietbart, insane performance artist Alex Jones, and agenda-driven Fox News, among others who discourage critical thinking in favor of following authoritarian pronouncements and foggy reasoning. Trump has become the leader of the fact-free world.

It's no surprise that Trump's supporters believe him when he slaps the "fake news" label on reality-based journalism about his administration's multiple scandals, obvious conflicts, deep corruption, and gross incompetence. But as long as his supporters refuse to think critically, Trump has no reason to even try to make sense.

Finding Common Ground on Immigration

June 2018

A video circulating in conservative social media shows former presidents Obama and Clinton talking about immigration in their State of the Union speeches. In 2013, Obama mentioned "strengthening border security." In 1995, Clinton said that many Americans "are rightly disturbed" about illegal immigration.

The intended point seems to be that Democrats are hypocrites for criticizing Donald Trump on immigration. Of course, that perspective ignores huge differences. Obama also talked about "establishing a responsible pathway to earned citizenship ... passing a background check and paying taxes and a meaningful penalty." And Clinton said we should focus on criminal immigrants and "cracking down on illegal hiring."

What true point is that both parties want to address problems with our immigration system. Democrats (and some sensible Republicans) have long supported practical policies. Both Clinton and Obama strengthened border security and focused on deporting undocumented immigrants with criminal records. Obama's DACA program provided a sensible and well-regulated path to citizenship for the most deserving young immigrants brought to the U.S. illegally as children.

John McCain and even George W. Bush attempted comprehensive immigration reform a decade ago. Unfortunately, hard-line Republican politicians blocked real reform and claimed that Democrats want "illegals" flooding into our country. That's simply a lie meant to stir anger and motivate anti-immigration sentiment.

Trump and his supporters now champion ineffective, expensive, xenophobic policies such as a border wall and mass deportation. And Trump's rhetoric has been dishonest and disgusting. He began his campaign with infamous accusations about Mexican rapists and recently lied by blaming Democrats for his own cruel policies that separate families, harm children, and fail to protect refugees fleeing violence.

Despite the current situation, there's hope. I recently joined a Republican friend in a Facebook discussion (prompted by the video of Obama and Clinton) that revealed common ground on immigration. My friend found Trump's rhetoric as unsettling as I do, but he generally agreed with Trump's policies because he claimed that undocumented workers were hurting him economically. As a construction subcontractor, he sees larger companies hire other subcontractors who use undocumented workers. He can't underbid crews with off-book, substandard wages.

I empathize with how unethical hiring impacts my friend's livelihood. That's clearly not fair. But I can't agree with his solutions. He claimed that the problem was caused by undocumented workers themselves, so they should all be arrested and deported.

My response was that far worse criminals reside much higher on the economic ladder: the companies that profit most from illegal jobs. General contractors have an ethical responsibility to ensure that subcontractors follow the law. The same ethics apply to any industry that uses illegal hiring practices. Lower costs and higher profits don't excuse ignoring obvious legal violations.

Here's a real-world example of how unethical companies profit from illegal hiring practices: In the early 1980s, a real estate mogul hired hundreds of undocumented construction workers at substandard wages. The mogul eventually settled a lawsuit over dangerous working conditions. Who reaped the profits from these hiring practices? That was a hypocrite name Donald Trump as his company cleared the site for Trump Tower. This is just one case that we know about. How many others have Trump's fixers buried?

People in poverty will do everything they can to provide for their families—including taking a risky journey to a wealthier country for illegal jobs. These folks are worthy of our empathy as well. But I can't relate to the Trumps of this world who hire undocumented workers so that they can afford to buy another golf course or live in gold-plated luxury.

These company officials made the choice to offer illegal jobs. Compared with undocumented immigrants desperate to work their way out of poverty, the CEOs are the real "illegals." To fight these criminals, we need comprehensive immigration reform that includes tougher laws and enforcement against companies that hire undocumented workers. Let's cage some corrupt CEOs in detention camps and see how quickly things change.

My Republican friend wasn't quite ready to scrap the wall and give up mass deportation just yet, but he was moving in that direction. He agreed that employers who abuse the immigration system for lavish profit should be prosecuted. Everyday Americans of every political affiliation agree that companies shouldn't profit from illegal hiring practices. We all need our elected representatives to focus on that agreement as well.

We all want our laws to discourage illegal immigration. That means not allowing companies to have a business model that relies on illegally exploiting undocumented workers rather than hiring Americans. If we prosecute the companies that hire illegally, then those illegal jobs will dry up. People won't come illegally for nonexistent jobs. The government could then focus on arresting and deporting the small percentage of undocumented immigrants who are actual criminals since the workers won't be drawn here any longer.

Moving forward, we should all work for a major shift in the immigration debate toward common ground. Both parties need to focus on what's right for American workers. Democrats need better messaging about their pro-worker policies, and Republicans need to abandon nasty rhetoric and feckless policies.

If my Republican friend and I can find solid agreement about prosecuting illegal employers, then our nation should be able to bring that perspective to our public policy.

Trump is the Real "Fake News"

July 2018

Less than a week after five people were murdered at the *Capital Gazette* newspaper, Donald Trump again used the term "fake news" in a tweet. That's disgusting.

Trump's definition of "fake news" is, of course, anything that doesn't match his agenda. For example, he calls coverage of the investigation into his Russia connections, "fake news." He labels any news network not named Fox or any outlet that questions his authoritarianism, "fake news."

Trump's supporters mimic his "fake news" catchphrase. They echo Richard Nixon's followers repeating his "liberal media" attacks decades ago. The resemblance extends to shouts of "Lügenpresse" ("lying press") in mid-Twentieth-Century Germany. In fact, Trump's supporters used that term at an October 2016 rally.

How can we sort "fake" from "real"? A great tool is blogger Vanessa Otero's "Media Bias Chart." Otero analyzed dozens of outlets and placed them on a horizontal axis of liberal to conservative bias, as well as a vertical axis of accuracy in reporting. Outlets near the top of the factual axis and the middle of bias axis are the most "real" news, while those in the chart's bottom corners are the most "fake."

The least biased, most factual outlets include AP, Reuters, NPR, BBC, and the major broadcast television news networks. The most fact-based outlets that skew slightly liberal include two Trump targets, *The New York Times* and *The Washington Post*, along with more liberal outlets such as *Democracy Now*, *The Nation*, and *Vox*. On the somewhat conservative, factual side are *The Economist*, *The Hill*, and the *National Review*, among others. These all constitute "real" news.

Trump's favorite target, CNN, occupies an odd spot on the chart as only slightly liberal (to the right of MSNBC) and middling for accuracy. The limited accuracy placement seems due largely to CNN's "roundtable" tradition of pitting partisan commentators against one another to generate ratings. The conservatives' inaccuracies cancel out the liberal pundits' facts.

CNN used to blanket viewers with every Trump campaign rally but now calls out Trump's many lies. That constitutes "real" news, but the network's evolving focus on fact-checking inspired Trump's most shameful attack, calling CNN and other reliable outlets, "the enemy of the American people."

Otero's chart is most interesting at its extremes. The fact-challenged, conservative-biased side includes *Drudge*, *The Daily Caller*, *Newsmax*, *Red State*, and, of course, Fox News. The worst right-wing offender is *InfoWars*, domain of conspiracy-monger Alex Jones. Sadly, a large percentage of conservatives claim that these biased, inaccurate sources provide the only "real" news in the media. Many Republicans get most of their "news" from these terrible outlets and dismiss accurate reporting and fact-checking as hopelessly liberal.

The opposite is true for the left. Some liberal outlets rank slightly below the middle for accuracy: *Huffington Post*, *BuzzFeed*, and *Daily Kos*, for example. Liberals know these are liberal publications. We read them, but we double-check their claims with nonbiased, fact-based sources.

I barely recognize the extreme liberal outlets that rank lowest in factual accuracy. *Patribotics*? Never heard of it. I've seen *Palmer Report* on Facebook, but I ignore their clickbait sensationalism. I don't know any liberals who take these sources seriously.

No major Democratic politician courts *Patribotics* or *Palmer Report*. But Trump constantly parrots Fox News, has been a guest on *InfoWars*, and has well-documented ties to the alt-right Breitbart.

Another troubling trend is that conservative media begins with their right-wing agenda and then shapes reporting, debate, and opinion toward that agenda. By contrast, liberal and responsible mainstream outlets strive to report facts, focus their debate on facts, and present editorial opinions based on facts.

Consequently, conservatives gobble up a steady diet of misinformation masquerading as news while they demonize legitimate journalism. Liberals might dabble in left-agenda-driven media but rely on nonpartisan sources to verify information for accuracy. That's a significant difference.

Otero's chart omits three important resources: *PolitiFact*, *FactCheck*, and *Snopes*. Along with *The Washington Post* fact-checker, these four are the go-to sources for assessing accuracy in the media and politics. *The Washington Post*, for example, has documented an astonishing 3,000-plus lies from Trump less than a year and a half into his presidency.

Conservatives generally dislike these fact-checkers because conservative politicians and pundits lie far more often than liberals. For example, compare *PolitiFact's* assessments of Barack Obama, Hillary Clinton, and Trump. Obama and Clinton are basically truthful three-fourths of the time. Trump, conversely, lies three-fourths of the time. The same general pattern holds for comparisons between Democrats and Republicans in general. Republicans are far less honest, yet their voters tolerate, celebrate, echo, and elect these liars.

To make matters worse, social media amplifies conservative misinformation. Trump on Twitter is as blatant a liar as he is behind a microphone. And the Russian election interference (which Trump calls "fake news" despite confirmation by the international intelligence community) was spearheaded on Facebook.

Ironically, Trump supporters who were hoodwinked by the Russians believe their views reflect independent thinking. They get most of their information from Russian troll-bots or biased right-wing outlets—two sources that push almost identical viewpoints. They believe our free press (protected by the First Amendment) is their enemy.

A recent Oxford University study showed that Trump supporters were more likely to spread Russian propaganda than anyone else. A pathological liar such as Trump wields power because he's enabled by a flock of pathological believers.

The free press—including the good people at the Capital Gazette—isn't "fake news." Trump is. We can succumb to Trump's attacks or we can embrace the First Amendment's protection of "real" news. Let's choose the Constitution.

Most Trump Supporters Aren't Evil People

August 2018

Fox News host Tucker Carlson recently claimed that Democrats don't care about Americans. In a better world, people like Carlson would be ignored. But in our flawed world, millions of Americans listen to him, so it's worth examining his rhetoric.

"For more than one hundred years," Carlson said on his show recently, "the Democratic Party was organized around the interest of ordinary Americans." That's generally true if you ignore the first fifty of those years when no political party cared much about ordinary Americans who weren't straight, white, Christian males.

For just a moment, Carlson sounded like a secret liberal ready to confess to his conservative audience: "Democrats ran campaigns for things like higher wages, better working conditions, against the banks that crushed their voters with debt."

Then he returned to his usual nonsense: "To the modern Democratic Party, Americans are an afterthought. Try to find a Democrat running this year on the opioid crisis, high energy prices, the collapse of public schools, the decline of the middle-class. Hard to find one."

If Carlson can't find any Democrats running on these issues, then his internet is disconnected. Every Democrat in America is running on exactly these issues. Go to any Democratic candidate's website, and you'll find these issues prominently displayed. Look up any Democrat's campaign speech, and these issues will be highlighted—along with other ways government can serve everyday Americans.

Carlson wants us to believe that Democrats are exclusively anti-Trump but not for anything. That's absurd. Democrats are anti-Trump precisely because his incoherent policies have one thing in common: instead of everyday Americans, they favor corporations and the wealthy. Carlson pretends that running against Trump and running for everyday Americans are different. They're not. They're identical.

Does Carlson actually believe his own pronouncements? Astonishingly, Carlson claims to be a Democrat. "I'm registered with a party that I sincerely despise," Carlson said in a bonkers interview

85

with Business Insider in 2017. He also claimed that he doesn't vote for president, but always votes "for the more corrupt [mayoral] candidate" because they won't upset his wealthy existence by doing something that might help ... wait for it ... everyday Americans. By his own standards, Carlson is the only registered Democrat who considers his fellow Americans, "an afterthought."

Carlson's recent tirade also included the claim that Democrats focus on immigration only because the party wants "open borders" to flood the country with Democratic voters. "Immigration is really the only issue that matters to them because packing the electorate is the only way to regain control of this country."

Trump himself claimed just weeks after he lost the popular vote by nearly three million votes that he, "won the popular vote if you deduct the millions of people who voted illegally." My response was, "Prove it, butthead" (only I didn't say "butthead"). Trump has yet to respond.

Every reputable study has shown no evidence of mass illegal voting. Yet Republicans embrace this falsehood as tightly as their "open borders" lie. Illegal immigration was actually down during President Obama's term, a fact verified by dozens of credible sources.

No Democrat has ever proposed anything resembling open borders. Instead, Democrats support comprehensive immigration reform that includes border security. Yet Trump, Carlson, and their right-wing comrades continue to lie about the subject, and their supporters continue to believe these lies.

Democrats actually care about immigration because comprehensive immigration reform would eliminate corporate reliance on immigrant labor and raise wages for everyone, especially Americans. Also, Trump's immigration policies are cruel, immoral, destructive, and a violation of the American ideal that our nation is a beacon for oppressed people everywhere. These facts aren't difficult to understand.

When Carlson lies about immigrants invading the country, he's mimicking white supremacist rhetoric. He's trying to make his older, white viewers believe the ridiculous theory that Democrats oppose Trump's immigration policies so that undocumented immigrants will march straight to the nearest polling places and vote illegally for Democrats.

Consequently, millions of otherwise fine people who watch Carlson, particularly those older white viewers alarmed by decades of Republican scare tactics, embrace white supremacists views they would normally find repulsive and anti-American. These folks aren't white supremacists by any stretch, but that's how they get tricked into siding with the Charlottesville tiki-torch jerks we all condemned (well, Trump, not so much).

Yes, some Trump supporters are hateful jerks. The hateful ones celebrate separating families at the border; wear t-shirts with the words, "Rope, tree, journalist, some assembly required"; compare protesters to speedbumps; call Elizabeth Warren, "Pocahontas"; and live to "piss off the libs." But, at heart, most Trump supporters aren't evil people and don't naturally hate immigrants or Democrats. They help their neighbors, hug their kids, do their jobs, and love our country—just as the vast majority of immigrants and Democrats in this country do.

Unfortunately, the non-evil Trump supporters are victims of the dishonest stories woven by jerks like Carlson and his ilk. These misinformation mongers dig deep to find the fear in their audience and weaponize it into hate. The target is anyone who threatens the authoritarian right-wing agenda—in this case, immigrants and Democrats.

Of course, the worst fear-to-hate transformer in the nation today is Trump himself. It's time to tell a better story about our nation, a story that appeals not to fear, but to the hope that we can rise up in the 2018 and 2020 elections and make Trump and his dishonest enablers "an afterthought."

America is Stronger than Trump

September 2018

My wife Betsy and I recently visited our nation's capital and gazed out at the skyline from our hotel's roof. We were struck by how the Washington Monument towered above the city as a reminder that this country has a powerful history and founding institutions to guide us and keep us focused on fundamental and evolving American values.

While in Washington, we explored the Smithsonian National Museum of American History. As we toured displays commemorating our presidents, I overhead a conversation between two women about my age.

"I love learning about presidents from my own lifetime," one woman said, "from Kennedy when I was a kid all the way to Obama."

"Remember Obama?" the other woman asked wistfully. "It seems like so long since we had a real president." The first woman nodded in agreement, and I found myself nodding as well.

When they noticed me, the first woman said, "Oh, I hope we didn't offend you."

"Not at all," I replied, and we shared the same forced laugh that I've exchanged with many kindred spirits during the past two years. "It's hard to believe we can be surrounded by all this presidential tradition, and then we have ... " I hesitated ... "you know who."

"How will we ever recover?" the second woman asked. It's a great question.

Of course, I recognize that no president is flawless. Carter and Obama are exceptions as people of strong character who ran nearly scandal-free administrations (despite what you hear on Fox News).

The glaring imperfections of most presidents are clear, especially in retrospect. Kennedy and Clinton had obvious sexual indiscretions. Johnson and Nixon were disastrously dishonest about the Vietnam War. Nixon, of course, also had Watergate, and Ford pardoned him. Reagan and Bush Sr. had Iran Contra. Bush Jr.'s general incompetence brought us the 9-11 attacks, two ill-conceived and mismanaged wars, and an economic crash.

Donald Trump, however, is different, to say the least. A full account of this unindicted co-conspirator's scandals would fill this newspaper for years. Instead, let's devote a few paragraphs to his malfeasance before and during his administration. (I'll have to use sentence fragments to save space.)

Conspiring with Russia to attack our elections. Groveling to Putin. Capitulating to Putin's agenda. Ignoring Russia's continued attacks on our election security. Praising and coddling murderous dictators across the globe, especially the near-nuclear Kim Jong Un. Constantly insulting other countries, including our allies. Senselessly attacking NATO.

Firing James Comey and the witnesses to Comey's account of Trump's obstruction of the Russia inquiry. Pressuring the Justice Department and attacking the Special Counsel's investigation.

Calling Mexican immigrants "rapists" and white supremacists "fine people." Having a long history of racially charged remarks and actions, including being sued by the federal government for discriminatory real estate practices. Promoting the racist "birther" lie. Being accused of multiple sexual assaults and harassment.

Calling the press the "enemy of the American people." Insulting John McCain for being a P.O.W. and calling Elizabeth Warren "Pocahontas." Attacking Black athletes for exercising their First Amendment rights. Lying constantly about Hillary Clinton, Obama, and nearly every Democrat in America. Crashing the Paris and Iran agreements. Holding circus-like campaign-style rallies. Appointing unqualified, corrupt saboteurs to cabinet positions. Granting pardons outside the usual system as political favors.

Paying off a supermarket tabloid to keep its vault of Trump scandals hidden. Illegally facilitating pornstar and playmate payoffs right before the election. Openly violating the emoluments clause to enrich himself and his family. Profiting from the con artistry of Trump University and the criminal slush fund of the Trump Foundation. Hiring undocumented workers. Cheating nearly everyone he's done business with. Hiding his tax returns.

Championing deficit-deepening tax cuts for the wealthy. Punishing American consumers with destructive tariffs. Hiding essential information about the current controversial Supreme Court nominee, who thinks serving presidents are above the law.

Vacationing more often than any other president. Having multiple security clearance controversies among White House staff.

Discussing classified information at Mar-a-Lago and other non-secure Trump properties. Trolling the world with his nasty Twitter addiction. Using unsecured cell phones and personal email (email!) to conduct government business.

Botching the response to Puerto Rico's hurricane. Separating families of asylum seekers at the border and failing to comply with legal rulings to reunite those families. Banning people from Muslim countries from entering the country. Proposing a ban on transgendered people in the military.

Whew! This list doesn't even include the revelations in Bob Woodward's upcoming book about Trump's insane presidency. And I'm sure I've missed other scandals because there are just too many to hold in a single human brain at one time.

When Obama was president, my Republican friends often lamented, "He's destroying America!" I responded by asking why they thought America was so weak that a single president could destroy our nation. They never had a good response.

Trump can't destroy our American institutions, no matter how hard he tries. He's clearly horrible, and we'll need decades to reverse his damage. But the Washington Monument looms over him. The Smithsonian keeps a record of our country at its best and at its worst. American is stronger than Trump.

One institution in particular offers the best remedy for recovering from Trump's madness: our elections. The midterms this year offer the choice between Democrats who still believe in American institutions, or Republicans who have become the "Cult of Trump" enabling his assault on our bedrock values.

And if Trump somehow evades responsibility for his many misdeeds, the next remedy will be booting him from our capital city in the 2020 election.

Brett Kavanaugh Disqualified Himself

October 2018

When I was in college forty years ago, our dorm rooms were tiny, barely able to hold matching pairs of tiny beds, closets, and desks. After a date, there was nowhere to sit comfortably except on the bed. For a shy kid like me, that was awkward. But for some of my classmates, those rooms could be dangerous.

During my freshman year, stories about women being drugged or pressured into drinking and "taken advantage of" (read: "raped") were common. One such incident happened in my dorm in one of those tiny rooms. I overheard some of the creeps involved bragging about it the next day.

Shortly after one guy brought a young woman home after a night at the bar, several of his male friends arrived, exposed themselves, and demanded sexual service from the woman. The guy telling the story laughed about how she cried, screamed, vomited, and eventually escaped after what must have been terrifying moments. And she left the college for good a week later.

Consider Brett Kavanaugh, a man accused of something painfully similar to what happened a few dorm rooms away my first year in college and in countless settings across this country every day. First, we saw Christine Blasey Ford's courageous, dignified testimony as she described her ordeal and positively identified Kavanaugh as her attacker.

Then we saw Kavanaugh's unhinged testimony. From the beginning, he was resentful and accusatory with a script that could have been lifted from an alt-right website. He spewed conspiracy theories about Democrats, ascribed his predicament to anger about Trump's election, and even blamed "the Clintons"—all while repeating "I like beer" enough times to invent a new drinking game.

Then he destroyed his own credibility by lying repeatedly under oath. He lied about seemingly small things, such as obvious sexual and alcohol references in his high school yearbook.

He lied about bigger things, such as the legacy connection that helped him get into Yale, the extent of his own drinking, the legal drinking age when he was young, and calling his friend Mark

Judge's book "fictionalized" even though it's a nonfiction memoir with a stumbling-drunk character named "Bart O'Kavanaugh."

And he lied about very significant things, such as repeatedly claiming that witness statements prove his innocence (they don't). These lies compounded his past dishonesty under oath when he lied about materials stolen by Republican operatives from Senate Democrats and his role in Bush administration policies on enemy combatants, judicial nominations, and wiretapping.

When asked about the FBI investigating, Kavanaugh evaded, ranted, and accused Democrats of ruining his life. Those aren't the actions of an innocent person. He repeated that he would "do whatever the committee wanted," knowing that the Republican-controlled committee planned no further investigation and a quick confirmation vote.

This was Kavanaugh when he had every motivation to be at his best. He was applying for lifetime promotion to the nation's highest court. Instead of presenting himself as a rational, thoughtful, empathetic person of integrity, he was a rageful, dishonest, rambling, entitled, jerk. Seeing Kavanaugh like this, sober and in public, we could easily picture the combative, violent drunk that several of his classmates remember.

It's worth noting that Hillary Clinton, the actual target of numerous fact-free conspiracies, testified before hostile Republican Congressional committees without Kavanaugh-style lying, crying, or erupting. His meltdown and her grace under pressure should retire forever the falsehood that women are too emotional for leadership positions.

Irony can be magical, but sometimes it's just plain nasty. For example, we have a president accused of sexual assault selecting a Supreme Court nominee who is also accused of sexual assault. And in a deeper irony, Kavanaugh might join Clarence Thomas (accused of sexual harassment decades ago) as the deciding votes to criminalize women's reproductive choices. In this case, irony sucks.

In a better world, someone who displayed Ford's courage and character would be our Supreme Court nominee, and Kavanaugh would be referred to Alcoholics Anonymous and mandatory anger-management classes. He should be reevaluated for his present court position, not considered for promotion.

Because Republicans control the Senate, Kavanaugh was on the verge of confirmation for weeks. During the hearing, frankly, they cowered behind prosecutor Rachel Mitchell to keep from looking like bullies during Ford's testimony. When Mitchell wasn't partisan enough for their purposes, they emerged from hiding to enable and amplify Kavanaugh's attacks.

Democrats fought for an FBI investigation until one Republican finally relented, but that investigation was so limited that it was practically useless. Meanwhile, almost all Republicans continued to rush someone to the bench who displayed, at best, biased views, dishonesty, and poor judicial temperament. At worst, he showed a criminal disregard for women as human beings. The drunken abusers from my college dorm don't belong on the Supreme Court, and neither does Kavanaugh.

This is probably not the last fight over inappropriate Supreme Court nominees—or terrible Republican proposals and regressive presidential policies. The best way to ensure the future pursuit of justice is to sweep the current Republican majorities out of Congress. That can only happen if good people cast wise votes this November.

Fear and Hope in 2018

November 2018

There's a reason Election Day closely follows Halloween. Halloween is the day we indulge our fears. Election Day is the day we indulge our hopes. Unfortunately, Republican politicians have tried to extend the pretend fear of Halloween into a real-life fright-fest on Election Day.

As the 2018 midterms approached, Republicans stoked the fear of what they call a "mob" marching on our southern border to "invade" our country. Trump said he would deploy up to 15,000 active-duty troops to the border (more than our current troops in Iraq and Afghanistan combined), despite the fact that the military officially deemed the "caravan" no criminal or terrorist threat.

Trump's border-deployment scheme is a shameful political stunt exploiting our troops at taxpayers' expense. Every reputable fact-checker has noted that Republican claims about the caravan are absurd. In reality, these are refugees fleeing violence in their own countries, drawn by hope for asylum and a better life in the United States.

Just a week before the election, Trump released a fearful ad reminiscent of the infamous "Willie Horton" ad of 1988. Trump's ad blamed Democrats for allowing a leering "illegal immigrant" who killed two police officers to stay in the country. The ad was so offensive that even Trump's favorite network, Fox News, stopped airing it the day before the election.

In reality, this particular criminal entered the country illegally and was deported during both the Clinton and G.W. Bush administrations. He was even released from jail by Republican sheriff Joe Arpaio, a Trump pardon recipient. Despite these facts, Trump still tells voters that Democrats want illegal immigrants to murder Americans. In reality, multiple studies show that native-born Americans murder and commit crimes at a higher rate than immigrants, legal or illegal.

Trump and his Republican enablers want their fear campaign to distract from recent horrific crimes connected to right-wing propaganda. The "MAGA-Bomber," a radicalized white Trump supporter, sent explosives to Democrats that Trump constantly attacks in speeches and social media. Another radicalized white man who believed that Jewish people were financing Trump's made-up "caravan invasion" murdered eleven Jewish worshippers at Temple. These horrible criminals were propelled by the Trump Train, not the caravan.

Another way that Republicans promote fear is their campaign against so-called "voter fraud," which actual research shows is an infinitesimal problem that doesn't influence election results. Trump claims (with no evidence) that he only lost the popular vote in 2016 because of millions of "illegal votes." That's complete nonsense, of course.

Wherever Republicans are in charge of elections, they exploit voter fraud fear to restrict voting by Americans they don't like. They study the voting behaviors of African-Americans, Hispanic-Americans, Native Americans, immigrants, women, and students, and then they try to keep their votes from counting.

During this election cycle, Republican moved or eliminated polling places in areas with a large percentage of Democratic voters, rejected registrations and absentee ballots for inconsequential discrepancies, demanded previously unrequired documentation for voting, provided faulty voting machines, and limited early voting options in many states with pivotal elections, including Georgia, Kansas, Texas, North Carolina, Florida, and North Dakota.

Add to these voter suppression tactics the Republican-led "Gerrymandering," which, along with the Electoral College, functions as an affirmative-action program for less qualified Republicans. Top it off with Republican denial about continuing Russian attacks on our elections and, by any reasonable measure, Republicans cling to power by cheating.

Yet another fear-based lie pushed by Republicans before the midterms was that Democrats are endangering health-care reform protections for people with pre-existing conditions. Republicans must think Americans have the shortest memories in the animal kingdom because Democrats actually passed those protections over the strenuous objections of Republicans in 2011. Those same Republicans are still trying to cut those protections even as they claim to be protecting them. The absurdity of this lie is mind-boggling, even by Republican standards for dishonesty.

So what's the alternative to Republican-stoked fear of goblins, monsters, immigrants, and Democrats? The other option, of course, is voting with hope. Thankfully, that's exactly what the majority of Americans did in last week's election.

Many in the media downplayed the results, but hope soundly defeated fear by millions of votes around the country. Progressive ballot measures passed in many states. Democrats flipped a significant number of state legislatures and governorships. The Senate is still close even after Democrats had to defend nearly three times as many seats as Republicans. And, best of all, Democrats will control the House of Representatives by a solid margin.

A Democratic House means that Trump's fearmongering can't be weaponized into federal law or financed in the federal budget. It means Democrats will control House committees and set the agenda for legislative proposals to help all Americans, not just their wealthy corporate donors. And it means the Speaker of the House, third in line to the presidency, won't be a Trump enabler.

The 2018 election gives us hope for America's future, particularly leading into the 2020 presidential election. A great start would be newly elected Democratic governors and legislators enacting state-level reforms to combat Republican attacks on health care and voting. Even better, by next Halloween, the new Democratic majority in the House can bring hopeful oversight to the fear-based abuses of the Trump administration.

Two Weeks that Define Trump's Presidency

December 2018

The period between the recent midterm elections and Thanksgiving was the most disturbing of the insane Trump presidency. Trump counts on "scandal fatigue" as each disgrace is quickly submerged in the wake of his next debacle, but we need to remember each misdeed before it sinks into the depths of history. Here's a summary of Trump's recent follies:

November 5: Without evidence, Trump raged against voter fraud on the eve of the midterm elections.

November 6: On election night, Trump tweeted, "Tremendous success tonight." In the end, Democrats dominated Republicans 53-45% in House races and 58-40% in Senate races. One party was "tremendous," but it wasn't Trump's.

November 7: Trump threatened House Democrats not to investigate him. He held a press conference where he insulted reporters, accused an African-American reporter of a "racist question," and attacked defeated Republicans for not sufficiently supporting him. He fired Attorney General Jeff Sessions and installed Matt Wittaker, an unqualified partisan under fraud investigation who has attacked the Mueller investigation.

November 8: Trump suspended Jim Acosta's press credentials, and his administration released a doctored video falsely claiming that Acosta had assaulted a White House intern.

November 9: Reports surfaced that Trump personally directed hush-money payments to his mistresses leading up to the 2016 election. Trump claimed, "I don't know Matt Whitaker," despite saying on national television in October, "I know Matt Whitaker."

November 10: Trump skipped a WWI ceremony in France due to rain. Rather than sympathizing with California wildfire victims, Trump falsely blamed state forest management and threatened to halt disaster funding.

November 11: French President Macron blasted Trump's brand of "nationalism" as a "betrayal of patriotism." For the second year in a row, Trump didn't go to Arlington National Cemetery on Veterans Day.

November 12: Trump baselessly claimed that vote counting in Florida should stop because the election was "massively infected." Despite often taking credit for stock market gains, Trump blamed a recent dip on Democrats.

November 13: CNN sued Trump over Acosta's credentials, and Maryland sued Trump over Whitaker's potentially unconstitutional appointment. Trump insulted Macron and France and blamed the Secret Service for him skipping the WWI ceremony.

November 14: Trump ridiculously claimed that people with "no right to vote … go to their car, put on a different hat, put on a different shirt, come in and vote again." He nonsensically claimed that people need voter ID to buy cereal.

November 15: Trump tweeted that he knew the "inner workings" of the Mueller investigation (which would be illegal), claimed that the investigation is "absolutely nuts," and "a total witch hunt like no other in American history!" Trump then nominated a handbag designer to an ambassadorship.

November 16: Trump, who won't meet with Mueller, said he (not his lawyers) wrote responses to Mueller's questions, greatly increasing his risk of perjury if those answers include his usual lies. The courts ordered Acosta's credentials reinstated. Trump awarded the Presidential Medal of Freedom to the wife of a casino owner who donated hundreds of millions of dollars to Trump and other Republicans.

November 17: When asked if California's wildfires changed his radical climate-change denial, Trump rambled, "No, no. I have a strong opinion. I want a great climate."

November 18: After touring fire-ravaged Paradise, California, Trump called the city, "Pleasure," adding, "what a name!"

November 19: CIA reports contradicted Trump and concluded that Saudi Prince Mohammed bin Salman ordered the assassination of journalist Jamal Khashoggi. Trump called Congressional Democrat Adam Schiff, "Little Adam Schitt" and criticized Admiral Bill McRaven, the Navy Seal who led the bin Laden raid. Trump claimed that Finland prevents fires by "raking" the forest, which the Finnish president denied saying.

November 20: Trump sided with the Saudis over American intelligence agencies in a widely condemned statement absolving bin Salman for killing Khashoggi, writing, "maybe he did and maybe he didn't!" A report indicated that Ivanka Trump used private email for government business, something Trump called criminal when Hillary Clinton did it. Another report indicated that Trump repeatedly urged the Justice Department to prosecute Clinton and James Comey. A federal judge blocked Trump's plan to deny asylum applications at the border.

November 21: Trump attacked the judges who ruled against his border polices, earning a rare rebuke from Supreme Court Chief Justice John Roberts. Trump melodramatically responded that rulings against him would cause "bedlam, chaos, injury and death."

November 21: Trump threatened a government shutdown if Congress doesn't fund his border wall.

November 21: Despite Khashoggi's murder, Trump enthusiastically thanked Saudi Arabia for lower oil prices. Then, disregarding his own administration's report on the dangers of climate change, Trump ignorantly tweeted, "Whatever happened to Global Warming?" because it was cold in the northeast.

November 22: Trump, who hasn't visited our troops in combat zones, politicized his Thanksgiving call to military members by criticizing judges, demonizing migrants, and boastfully naming himself as something he was thankful for on Thanksgiving.

Perhaps no other period defines this radical, incompetent, and corrupt president more completely. Trump had hundreds of previous scandals and will have far more before he leaves office. We need to remember them all and respond accordingly. The midterms were a good start. Let's keep going and elect a real president in 2020.

Why Do Trump Supporters Ignore
his Disrespect for our Military?

January 2019

Author's Note: This essay is the original version of the January 2019 column before I had to cut a third of it for the newspaper's word-count limit. Trump's disrespect for our military is so extensive that I wanted to reflect the extent of his malice in this book with the more comprehensive version. And all of this happened long before news surfaced in September 2020 that Trump had insulted soldiers who had died in battle as "suckers" and "losers." His supporters, of course, blamed the media.

Back in 2010, one of my students approached me after the final class of the semester. He was in his late twenties, and I knew from his presentations in class that he came from a military family—although he hadn't enlisted himself. He respectfully asked if we could talk about something that was bothering him.

"Of course," I replied.

"Well, I Googled your name the other day, and I found out something disturbing." I hoped it wasn't some of my bad poetry or pictures of my mop-top hair in college. He continued. "I found some of the things you wrote, and it looks a little like you're a liberal." He whispered the last word.

"I am," I replied. My teaching style focuses on helping students develop their own critical thinking skills rather than political indoctrination, and I try to model how critical thinking can lead to informed and reasonable viewpoints.

He looked a bit shocked. "Really? You're admitting it?"

"Yes," I said with a chuckle. "What's wrong with being a liberal?"

"Liberals hate the troops," he said without hesitation.

"No," I said gently. "Liberals support our military as much as everyone else in this country."

"That's not what I read," he replied. "I just saw online that Obama is cutting soldiers pay. How can he do that if he supports the troops?"

Always looking for that "teachable moment," I popped open my laptop and asked him to find the reports on Obama cutting military pay. He directed me to his uncle's Facebook page where we found a post from a website with a name something like, "American Patriots for America," that made the claim that "our so-called president" was cutting military pay while "massively bumping up welfare."

"This is interesting," I said. "Remember when we talked about issues like reasonable tone and fact-checking when we covered persuasion speeches in class? Does 'so-called president' sound reasonable? And did you fact-check this claim?"

"No," he replied. "But this is just Facebook. I thought all that stuff was just for this class."

"Being reasonable and factual is important in any kind of communication," I said. "Let's see what we can find on this issue."

We spent about five minutes researching the subject and discovered that Obama had actually proposed a pay increase for the military. In fact, he proposed the exact amount required by law, tied to the U.S. Labor Department's Economic Cost Index.

"Why did my uncle lie about this?" my student asked.

"I don't think your uncle meant to lie," I said. "He just didn't fact-check. But the people doing the website where he got the information are lying to push some kind of agenda about how liberals hate the troops. We don't. We just don't want to see the military used to push agendas that aren't good for the country or the world."

"I'll be honest," he said. "This blows my mind.

"In a good way?" I asked.

"I'm not sure," he replied. He shook my hand and left for summer vacation.

Nearly a decade has passed since that conversation. I haven't seen or heard from that student again, but I've often wondered if our brief fact-check influenced the way he communicates about political issues.

For example, I'm curious about what he thinks of Donald Trump's recent claims about military pay increases. While making his first visit to our troops in a combat zone over the holidays, Trump told our troops that he got them "one of the biggest pay raises you've ever received ... You haven't gotten one in more than ten years ... Make it ten percent. Make it more than ten percent."

Like so much of what he says, every word of Trump's claim is an outright lie. And because he lied directly to our troops serving in a combat zone, it's one of the most disgusting lies he's ever told.

And this is not the first time that Trump has told a similar lie. He made the "first time in ten years" claim in May 2018 to a group of military spouses and mothers. Someone must have told him that this claim is wrong, but he repeated it anyway. Imagine if Obama had twice told such a lie to soldiers and their families? In that case, Republicans would actually have been justified in claiming that he "hates the troops."

But Republicans have given Trump a free pass when it comes to his history of disrespecting and attacking the military that dates back to his young adulthood. His avoidance of the Viet Nam draft through five deferments has been well documented, including reports of his likely fictional "heel spurs."

Trump also claimed he was the beneficiary of a high draft number, but that claim contains clear falsehoods. Trump says he learned of his high draft number as he watched the draft lottery on television while he was a student at the Wharton School of Finance, but that lottery was held eighteen months after he graduated.

Despite avoiding service in Viet Nam, Trump has made comments that show deep disrespect for those who fought in that war. In 1998, Trump agreed with shock-jock Howard Stern that avoiding STDs while sleeping around was his own version of going to Viet Nam and said he deserved a Congressional Medal of Honor for the bravery of his promiscuity.

Trump implied that putting men and women together in the military leads to men being rapists and women being victims.

Trump has demeaned military training as well. He claimed that going to a military prep school gave him, "more training militarily than a lot of the guys that go into the military."

In his business life, Trump's fraudulent Trump University specifically targeted veterans in their scheme that eventually led to a $25 million judgment against Trump.

During his campaign, Trump insulted veterans and military members several times. His nasty criticism of John McCain ("I like people who weren't captured") would have ended the campaign of any other candidate. Instead, many Republicans turned on McCain, a genuine hero, instead of Trump.

Trump has repeatedly lied about opposing the Iraq War and mostly showed a limited understanding of the issues as that war unfolded. He even claimed that American soldiers stole millions of dollars during the Iraq War.

Trump attacked Khizr and Ghazala Khan, whose son was killed during the Iraq War in 2004, for criticizing him at the Democratic National Convention.

Trump reinforced the stigma against veterans who suffer from PTSD by saying that some soldiers "are strong" while others "can't handle" their traumatic military experiences.

In 2016, Trump skipped a debate to hold a "fundraiser" for veterans. In fact, the event was more of a campaign rally, and half of the money raised went immediately to the Trump Foundation, which has since been closed down for what former New York Attorney General Barbara Underwood called, "a shocking pattern of illegality." Only after repeated pressure from the media did Trump actually donate the money raised at the rally to military charities.

Trump showed no understanding of or respect for military traditions when a veteran offered him his Purple Heart (awarded when a service member is wounded in combat), and Trump said, "I always wanted to get the Purple Heart. This was much easier."

As President, Trump has continued to disrespect our troops in a number of ways. Barely a week into his term, Trump approved a disastrous military rain in Yemen that led to the death of a Navy Seal. Had a Democratic president made such an obvious blunder, no doubt Congressional Republicans would still be holding hearings and demanding answers, much as they did after the Benghazi incident. Instead, they've been largely silent on Trump's early term debacle.

When Trump was asked about why he didn't reach out to the family of Army Sergeant La David Johnson after Johnson was killed while on a mission against terrorists in Africa, Trump dishonestly claimed that President Obama and other presidents didn't contact the relatives of fallen soldiers.

When Trump finally did call Myeshia Johnson, Sergeant Johnson's pregnant widow, he had trouble remembering the soldier's name and said that Sergeant Johnson, "knew what he signed up for" when he enlisted in the military.

Trump skipped a ceremony to honor WWI veterans during a trip to France because of rain, and he later blamed the Secret Service for the omission.

Trump frequently attacks military leaders who disagree with him, including retired Admiral William McRaven, the leader of the mission that killed Osama bin Laden.

In a pre-midterm publicity stunt that used our soldiers as pawns, Trump deployed thousands of troops to our southern border when the Pentagon had determined that there was no actual threat at the border.

Trump talked about several controversial political issues during his Thanksgiving Day call to American service members, breaking the tradition of keeping politics out of honoring service members.

In December, after a series of incoherent policy initiatives, Trump tweeted an incoherent video stating that he would pull U.S. troops out of Syria. His decision shocked allies and delighted adversaries. His Secretary of Defense, General James Mattis, soon resigned over the issue, and Trump has flip-flopped on his plan ever since.

Considering Trump's terrible record, how do Republicans justify supporting a president who shows such hostility and disrespect toward the military? I'm guessing that many of them, like my student back in 2010, don't fact-check Trump's statements. When they do encounter evidence that Trump is lying, many simply dismiss the fact-checks as attacks by the liberal media who hate the military as much as they Trump.

But Trump's lie about military pay is about as obvious as it gets. No thinking person can claim that Trump was just exaggerating or that Democrats have told lies equal to this one. Trump is in his own league as a liar, with the Washington Post documenting more than 7,600 lies since he has been in office.

Trump's Oval Office speech last week was full of lies about immigration and border security. In other words, it was a typical Trump speech—just in a different setting. His supporters either don't have the ability to know the truth or they don't care.

Trump exposed himself as a pathological liar during the campaign, but too many pathological believers let him get away with it. The fact that they let Trump get away with lying about and to our military is a new low in hypocrisy.

What Do Democrats Stand For?

"Democrats don't stand for anything. They're just anti-Trump."

This sentiment has become a mantra for political pundits, so-cial-media mavens, and water-cooler philosophers. They repeat it so often that some people think of it as a "truism" or "conventional wisdom." In fact, there's nothing true or wise about this lie.

This 2018 midterm election was definitely a rebuke of Trump's corruption, incompetence, and terrible policies. But that election went far beyond a simplistic anti-Trump statement. It was a strong endorsement of Democratic initiatives.

Democrats across the country won the midterms because they campaigned on many important issues: improved access to health care; minimum wage increases; gun-safety regulation; smart border security; humane immigration policies; equal pay; infrastructure and manufacturing support; college affordability; education funding and reform; fair tax systems; Wall Street reform; jobs and job-training programs; diplomacy over war; support for veterans; criminal justice reform; LGBT rights; reproductive choice; drug law reform; support for Social Security, Medicaid, and Medicare; promotion of small business over corporations; a strong social safety net; health and safety regulations; and conversion to clean/green energy.

Considering that Trump and his supporters are either actively opposed to these initiatives or haven't done anything productive to support them, being anti-Trump also means favoring the Democrat's viewpoint. As J.M. Sorrell pointed out in her excellent recent column, other than feeling victimized and lashing out at liberals, today's "conservatives" haven't expressed a coherent viewpoint.

One of the biggest issues for Democrats is making government more accountable to the people. That's why Democrats in the House of Representatives are proposing their first major bill, HR1. The bill expands voting rights, cleans up campaign finance laws, and strengthens government ethics.

The part of HR1 that has gotten the most attention is the proposal to make Election Day a national holiday. Anyone who has rushed to vote or even skipped voting due to the demands of their job can relate to this proposal. But HR1 doesn't stop there. It also includes provisions for automatic voter registration, expanded early voting, prohibiting purging of voter rolls, recruiting and training more poll workers to cut down on voting wait time, and providing more election security, especially from attacks by foreign powers. Most important, HR1 puts redistricting in the hands of independent commissions to eliminate the partisan Gerrymandering that Republicans have used to sway elections for a decade.

HR1's campaign finance improvements include greater transparency of political contributions, particularly supporting the repeal of Citizens United, ending "dark money" secret funding of Super PACs, and prohibiting coordination between campaigns and Super PACs. The bill would also ensure transparency of donations by government contractors, as well as the disclosure of funding for political ads on social media. Another focus is reducing corruption by rewarding candidates who raise money through small donations rather than huge corporate funding. And to aid in the actual enforcement of election laws, the bill calls for increasing the membership of the Federal Elections Commission from four to five as a way to prevent partisan tied votes that lead to enforcement inaction.

And the ethical components of HR1 actually address the corrupt government "swamp" that Trump has made far swampier despite his campaign promise to the contrary. Presidential and Vice Presidential candidates would be required to release ten years of tax returns, codifying a tradition that Trump defied. HR1 would strengthen the Office of Government Ethics, provide greater oversight of lobbyists and foreign agents, and end the reprehensible practice of taxpayers funding sexual harassment or discrimination settlements against Congress members. The bill would also meet a long-overdue need by establishing a code of ethics for the Supreme Court, a branch of government that has never had a formal ethics structure.

How have Republicans responded to HR1? One byproduct of the Trump/Republican government shutdown has been a delay in work on any legislation. Republicans are happy to slow down any common-sense reforms proposed by Democrats.

Republicans have long made no secret of their contempt for government. Ronald Reagan himself infamously said, "Government is the problem." Their contempt for government extends to contempt for voting rights because they know that when more Americans vote, Democrats do better in elections.

Senate Majority Leader Mitch McConnell called the common-sense reforms of HR1 a "power grab" and a "sprawling proposal to grow the federal government's power over Americans' political speech and elections." McConnell's claims make no sense—unless he is afraid of putting power into the hands of voters. McConnell and his Republican colleagues should be required to explain to the American people why they don't fully support our right to vote.

The next time Republicans claim that Democrats don't have any ideas, please keep in mind that they're simply trying to distract from their own party's incoherence and terrible proposals. Yes, Democrats are anti-Trump, but that's because we are in favor of returning control of the government to voters instead of corporate donors, billionaires, lobbyists, and foreign adversaries. That's a position shared by most of the country, and it must terrify Trump and his enablers as they desperately try to hold onto power. The best way to make their worst fears come true is to vote for the Democratic agenda in 2020.

Tough Love for Trump Supporters

March 2019

This isn't John Sheirer. John's outside shoveling snow or clearing brush after the latest windstorm, or some other nonsense work that New Englanders have to do. Then he'll probably help some neighbors clear their driveways. Trump would call that "Socialism." That's his word for helping other people.

This is John's twin brother, Jack. I live in Florida where we never have to shovel snow, but our politicians shovel some pretty big loads of something else.

I'm what you might call John's "evil twin."

John tells me that the key to good column writing is being "reasonable." I've read his columns, and I can tell you that means being nice to people who do idiotic things. That's not my style.

While John's outside playing Boy Scout, I'll commandeer his column to say something to Trump supporters, so buckle up.

Hey, Trumpers! What's wrong with you?

Did you people see Michael Cohen on TV talking about your clown-haired Messiah? You know what that was? That was a henchman ratting out a mob boss—the gangster you voted for!

"But, Jack," you say, "Cohen's a liar." No kidding! That's why Trump loved him for years. And you had no problem with him lying to support your dinky-fingered dictator up until he flipped for the feds. You believed every twisted word Cohen spat out until he flipped. Heck, you guys even made him deputy finance chair of the Republican Party!

John tells me to have empathy and not attack Trumpers. John's an optimist. I'm a pissed-offtimist. When have you Trump supporters showed any empathy to anyone?

Here's all the empathy you'll get from me: I feel bad that you were fooled into voting for a third-rate con artist. Stop supporting a toxic man-baby, and maybe we can talk about more empathy. Until then, all you get is scorn and pity.

And you'll get some tough love, too. You claim to be against "political correctness." You claim that you want people to "speak their minds," but then you melt like snowflakes when someone questions your views." Well, here comes some questions. Ready? Here it is.

You know who didn't hire actual criminals for a presidential campaign or business? Hillary Clinton didn't. You know who was cleared of criminal activity by multiple investigations, including kangaroo courts led by Republicans? Hillary. You know who Trump lied about every day on the campaign trail? Hillary, again. You know who believed those lies? Look in the mirror.

You know whose foundation got shut down because it's a criminal slush fund? Not the Clinton Foundation, that's for damned sure. The criminal in question goes by the initials D.J.T. But Hillary sent some emails, so you screamed, "Lock her up!" and voted for an actual crook. Nice job.

You know who's already an unindicted co-conspirator in a felony and had a $25-million-dollar judgment against him for running a fake university? Here's a hint: He's also currently under investigation for conspiracy with a hostile foreign power, money laundering, insurance fraud, bank fraud, nepotistic security clearances, and corruption at his inauguration.

You know who didn't kiss up to dictators like Vladimir Putin or Kim Jong Un? Barack Obama didn't, and neither did Hillary.

You know who didn't shut down the government and declare a fake emergency over a stupid wall that would cost too much, not help with illegal activity at the entry points where drugs actually come into the U.S., and can be breached with a tunnel, ladder, airplane, drone, or really good pole vaulter? Nancy Pelosi didn't. In fact, she made Trump surrender repeatedly.

You know who actually has Native American ancestry? Elizabeth Warren does. Guess who's a racist for calling her "Pocahontas"? Trump is and so are you if you mimic him. You know who was born in America? Obama was. You know who only condemned white supremacists by reading from notes written by someone else as if he's a hostage reading a ransom note? That was your semi-literate hero to neo-Nazis. Who did the KKK officially endorse for president? Not Hillary, that's for damned sure. You know who's a racist for leading the "birther" movement? Trump ridiculously tried to blame Hillary, but that was him. That's all Trump—and it's you, too, if you don't condemn his racist crap.

You know who never bankrupted a casino, where the house is always supposed to win? No Democrat in any elected office ever. That was your business genius, Trump.

You know who bragged about grabbing women where every real man knows you shouldn't touch a woman without absolute consent? That was the guy so-called "conservative Christians" voted for in overwhelming numbers. Don't you people know Jesus watches you in the voting booth?

You know who will be back next month with another reasonable column? John will. Right now, he's outside yelling, "Hey, Jack! C'mon out! Shoveling snow is fun!" John even likes shoveling the thick piles at the end of the driveway after the snowplow goes by. Trump supporters would rather whine about the tyranny of those piles than be happy about the freedom of freshly plowed streets. Thank you, Socialist snowplows!

Overall, I guess there's a place for John's empathy and reasonable tone in today's political world. But sometimes we all need to voice our outrage. Hopefully, we can get in touch with both our reasonable and angry sides and fix the mess you Trumpers have made of our great country. If so, you'll never have to hear my nasty voice again.

Trump Keeps Using that Word

April 2019

In the beloved movie *The Princess Bride*, heroic Inigo Montoya says to babbling villain Vizzini. "You keep using that word. I do not think it means what you think it means." A real-life villain, Donald Trump, is currently making the same mistake with the word "exonerated."

Vizzini is a comic figure in the movie, but there's nothing funny about Trump's claim that the Mueller Report "exonerates" him. He's illustrating his own ignorance. Thus far, we've only seen a memo from Trump's hand-picked Attorney General, William Barr. Barr's memo is not the Mueller Report.

Barr makes the questionable claim that Trump did not commit obstruction of justice. The whole purpose of a Special Counsel is to lift the investigation above partisan politics, so Barr clearly has no business making judgments on the investigation's results.

First, Barr is a Trump appointee. Second, Barr auditioned for his current job with a memo opining that Trump shouldn't even be investigated for obstruction of justice. Third, Barr issued his decision two days after receiving the massive report, not nearly enough time for an open-minded assessment. Fourth, the branch of government constitutionally charged with presidential oversight is Congress, not Trump's Justice Department.

The results of independent investigations into Richard Nixon and Bill Clinton went to Congress, not to these presidents' appointees. Imagine if Nixon's administration minimized the Watergate investigation as Barr is doing with the Mueller Report. Republicans fumed when Bill Clinton had a brief, impromptu encounter with Attorney General Loretta Lynch while Hillary Clinton was running for president. The Trump administration is doing far worse now.

Despite his obvious bias, Barr actually notes that the Mueller Report includes evidence of obstruction by Trump. Mueller's report states that "while this report does not conclude that the President committed a crime, it also does not exonerate him." That's literally the opposite of Trump's ridiculous claim of "exoneration."

Barr also cherry-picks from Mueller to try to absolve Trump of Russian collusion by specifically quoting Mueller's assessment of the Trump campaign's connections with "the Russian government." Barr doesn't mention the many known contacts between Trump and Russians who may not be formally affiliated with the Russian government who operate under Putin's direction. Not many people thought that Trump texted Putin, "THX! KUTGW!" Crime bosses supply the overall vision. Their underlings do the detailed dirty work.

There is clear evidence in the public record that Trump and his campaign worked with Russians during and after the campaign. Donald Trump Jr., Paul Manafort, and Jared Kushner met with a Russian they thought was a government official to try to get dirt on Hillary Clinton. Manafort offered to brief a Russian oligarch on the Trump campaign, and he sent campaign polling data to another Russian. Trump publicly asked the Russians to hack Hillary Clinton's emails, and they tried to do so hours later. George Papadopoulos tried to arrange meetings between Trump and Putin during the campaign, and Kushner tried to set up a secret communications channel between Trump and Putin after the election. Roger Stone communicated with Wikileaks about the materials Russia hacked. Michael Flynn had secret communication with the Russian ambassador. And Trump himself had multiple secret business dealings with Russians dating back years and continuing through much of the presidential campaign.

And then Trump and his associates lied about all of these Russian connections during and after the campaign, both to the American people and, often, to the FBI. And no one from the Trump campaign reported the Russians to the FBI. None of this is anything close to the behavior Americans want from a president and his close associates.

The Barr memo also notes that Mueller confirms U.S. intelligence reports about Russian hacking and disinformation to attack our election. Trump has consistently denied Russia's attack, probably to avoid the obvious truth that he would have lost the election without Russian help. This aspect of Mueller's report is more evidence that Trump sides with Russia over America.

Trump has been colluding with Russia since he took office, from denying Putin's attack on our election, to undermining sanctions against Russia, to carrying Putin's water in opposing NATO. It's not a stretch to think Trump also colluded during his campaign.

Overall, Trump's presidency is what Vizzini would call, "inconceivable." Trump keeps forcing terrible policies on our country. He's currently in the process of stealing funds from our troops to build his wasteful and ineffective border wall, and he's attacking health care reform in ways that would strip insurance from millions of Americans and regress us to the days of rampant abuse by health insurance corporations.

As 2020 approaches, Democrats need a three-pronged approach to defeat Trump. First, obviously, fight the terrible Trump/Republican policies. Second, propose policies that help everyday Americans, as they've been doing with major initiatives such as election reforms and Obamacare fixes. And third, investigate the rampant corruption of Trump and his administration.

Trump's insane "exoneration" claims may be pushing the current media narrative. But the long-term message is clear: Trump is a horrible president in every way. When the full Mueller Report becomes public and other investigations proceed, the truth about Trump's high crimes and misdemeanors will be clear.

How Do We Respond to Gaslighters?

When I was a kid, I overheard some adults telling a strange story that went like this. It seems one of their friends heard several reports about her husband walking arm-in-arm with an unfamiliar woman. Then she found lipstick on her husband's shirt collar and a hotel receipt in his pocket for a day he said he was at work. When she confronted him, he quickly hung up the phone and claimed he was talking to "no one."

"Are you having an affair?" the woman asked.

"Did you witness me having sex with another woman?" her husband snapped.

"No," the wife replied.

"Well, then," the husband announced. "Thank you for proving that I've been faithful to you!"

The men laughed while the women grimaced. I was too young back then to understand "gaslighting" as practiced by liars and cheats. Now, with the help of the world's most famous adulterer, Donald Trump, I understand the point of the story. When confronted with the Mueller Report, Trump boasted, "No collusion! No obstruction!" in classic gaslighting fashion.

In fact, the Mueller Report shows how Russia acted to weaken the United States by supporting an unqualified, unstable, irresponsible, easily manipulated candidate. The report shows that Trump and his campaign welcomed Russia's help, lied about that help, and didn't report the election interference to American authorities.

Mueller's team declined to say that Trump's Russian connections rose to the level of a provable, criminal "conspiracy," but those connections are clearly damning to Trump and his campaign. The report also shows that Trump acted maliciously to undermine the investigations into the Russian election attack. Mueller's team didn't charge Trump with obstruction of justice only because he is a sitting president. If he weren't, he'd be indicted right now.

And yet the gaslighters are out in force, braying for Trump's innocence. How should we deal with these people as they deny basic reality?

For example, I have a coworker who floods Facebook with memes portraying Democrats as insanely attacking a heroic president. Many of his reposted memes (never original material because that would require original thinking) claim that Democrats see imaginary Russians around every corner. If my coworker had read the report, he would know that Mueller clearly destroyed Trump's talking point that Russia didn't attack our election. Other memes from this coworker depict Democrats driven by hatred and delusion rather than patriotism and evidence. And, of course, he posts fact-free, absurd memes twisting reality to blame Obama and Clinton for Trump's crimes.

How can I expect this guy to do his job when he can't see basic reality?

What about Attorney General William Barr? He has been lying about the Mueller Report since it was submitted. Barr claimed Mueller didn't find collusion, but the report details multiple inappropriate contacts between the Trump campaign and Russians, and Mueller made clear he was looking for criminal conspiracy, not collusion. Barr claimed that Mueller didn't feel bound by the guideline that a sitting president can't be indicted, but Mueller cited that exact guideline as part of the reason for not charging Trump. Barr claimed he had the right to pass judgment on the president's obstruction, but Mueller clearly left that for Congress to decide.

Hundreds of former Justice Department prosecutors (Republicans and Democrats from the Eisenhower to Trump administrations) recently signed a letter saying that Trump would be charged with obstruction of justice were he not a sitting president.

How can we have faith in our justice system when the attorney general's written statements, press conferences, and even Congressional testimony are incredibly dishonest?

And, worst of all, how should we deal with a president who denies the basic reality that he has been caught in a multi-layered web of lies, deceit, collusion, and obstruction? Trump can lie about the report, defy subpoenas, falsely claim executive privilege, and rail about "witch hunts" all he wants. That doesn't change the fact that he's unfit for any office, let alone the highest office in our nation.

What do we do as responsible citizens when we see Trump and his enablers deny basic reality in ways that damage the moral fabric of our country? How can we trust these self-serving liars to care about the nation's best interests? Do we take the easy path and accept their lies, shrugging our collective shoulders and ignoring evidence? Or do we take the difficult path and confront those who think a lie that benefits them is better than a truth that benefits us all?

Do we just dab some stain-remover on the collar and toss the cheater's shirt into the washing machine? Or do we dump his entire wardrobe into the street?

I say we dump the cheater and landslide him from our White House in November 2020. Once on the street, he won't be able to damage our country any further. And he won't be able to hide behind the temporary immunity of his office. That's when prosecutors should follow Mueller's roadmap and indict Trump for flagrantly obstructing our nation's justice system.

Gaslighting philanderers, terrible as they are, don't necessarily belong in jail. But criminal presidents absolutely do.

"Voices for Resistance"
Shows the Power of Community

June 2019

Writers can sometimes feel like isolated voices floating in the glow of a laptop screen. In a similar way, living through the Trump presidency has a way of making many of us ask, "Am I the only one who feels this way?" Fortunately, living in Western Massachusetts provides clear evidence that we're not alone as writers or as people striving to make the world a better place.

A recent event served as a superb reminder of the power of community, for both writers and resisters. "Voices for Resistance: A Celebration" brought together a wonderful group of "citizen writers" at Forbes Library on June 5, 2019. Fifteen readers, all members of the area writing group Straw Dog Writers Guild, shared diverse perspectives on what it means to resist the current degradation of what we love about humanity and our nation.

Andrea Hairston got the event off to a rousing start, sparkling the room with inspiring performance poems. She contrasted the celebration of humanity with the folly of those who would wall us all off as enemies.

Chivas Sandage explored the painful irony of life going on as normal while people are tortured around the world. And she contextualized that irony within the depiction of a president so childish that he fumes when his visit to Mara Lago is ruined by rain.

Christopher J. Sparks read from intense, perceptive journal entries about desperately but purposefully searching through these dark times—literally and figuratively—to find meaning in life.

Doug Anderson's poems brought lyrical, musical language that transformed the dehumanizing horrors of war into the surprising discovery of love in the aftermath of Vietnam.

Ilina Singh's poems centered on her native India, a place not so different from present-day America, where fear coexists with beauty, danger with family, nightmares with dreams.

Lanette Sweeney shared a stirring elegy to help rid us of the hate and dread of the 2016 election as we move toward a far more hopeful turnaround in 2020.

Maria Luisa Arroyo read multilingual, celebratory homages to great women poets while honoring the power and accomplishments of everyday women.

Mary Warren Foulk spoke of marrying her wife in Oregon in 2004, where marriage equality was briefly legal, only to have their marriage voided by a discriminatory ballot initiative. Her poems focused on the love within her marriage despite the senseless hate of strangers. Thankfully, the couple remarried here in Massachusetts where the credo, "love is love," has been law longer than anywhere else in the nation.

Marya Zilberberg reflected with soul-searching humor about living near her Trump-supporting neighbors, whose ignorance was emboldened by the 2016 election into an enigmatically misspelled lawn sign reading, "All Life's Matter."

Nicole M. Young read about how the hopes and expectations of youth are often met with the reality of inequality for those not born into privilege. Yet her voice persists, refusing to be silenced by oppression.

Patrick Donnelly read a poem of remembrance for friends who died of AIDS, and he reminded us that this terrible disease is still very much with us, mostly due to fear and discrimination.

Theresa Vincent finished the evening's readings by reflecting on the personal tragedy of violence against women while still affirming the unity and beauty of life.

For my part, I was planning to read from my fictional satire, "Donald Trump's Top Secret Concession Speech." The premise is that Trump developed the tiniest fragment of a conscience as the 2016 election approached and realized he'd be a terrible president. (Yep, it's fantasy.) Michael Moore says that humor is a key to resisting Trump, and that's a big part of why I wrote the book. If we're not laughing these days, we might start to cry.

But I've also heard that another way to resist is simply to add beauty to the world. With that in mind, I read a piece depicting one of the most beautiful events any human can experience: giving your dog a treat after she poops on a winter day. That's a beauty undimmed by the ugliness Trump and his enablers have amplified in our world.

The "Voices for Resistance" event was a welcome respite from Trump's constant assault on the aspirational American values of basic human dignity and equality. But those at the event also felt a call to action to keep resisting the authoritarianism, greed, and dehumanization that are very much central qualities of this presidency.

Best of all, the event was a reminder that, no, we are not the only ones who feel this way, whether here in Western Massachusetts or across the world. Sometimes we may feel alone, but we're definitely embraced by community. In these difficult times, we can all speak with the strength of our individual and common voices because we're all in this together.

Author's note: Straw Dog Writers Guild is a nonprofit, volunteer organization dedicated to supporting the writing community of Western Massachusetts by strengthening, engaging, and connecting writers at all levels of development. The group's website is strawdogwriters.org.

Time for the Grown-Ups

July 2019

If you turned on your television recently, you may have discovered a rare treat: grown-ups running for president! Yay! Two nights of debates featured a crowded field of Democrats. Each of them would make a better president than Donald Trump, but the standouts were Elizabeth Warren and Kamala Harris.

Warren dominated the "polite night." Her wonky, "I have a plan for that," professorial style perfectly complimented her folksy personality and clear commitment to representing everyday Americans. Trump's racist "Pocahontas" insults were blissfully absent during this debate because Democrats aren't racist jerks. And Warren didn't mention Trump once, proving that she's a formidable candidate in her own right, not just in contrast with the anomaly in the White House.

Last year, Warren was criticized for her ancestry reveal. But her results confirmed what her family told her growing up: She has Native American ancestry. She hasn't used that ancestry to gain unfair advantage in school, work, or politics—despite dishonest claims from Republican detractors.

Imagine Trump repeatedly tossing out his racist nickname during a general election debate against Warren. He'd look like a spoiled toddler next to a responsible adult. The only people who like Trump's insults are just as childish as he is. Everyone with any sense is justifiably horrified.

The second night of debates was feistier. Harris was able to stand out with a combination of toughness, optimism, and a personal storytelling style. The key moment occurred when Harris directly addressed Joe Biden regarding busing in the 1970s. As a young Senator, Biden opposed federally mandated busing while Harris, as a young child, benefited from the improved educational opportunity busing provided.

Harris showed guts confronting a beloved political icon, along with optimism that American government can be a force for good in our everyday lives. And she did so without giving Republicans ammunition against Biden, who may still be the nominee looking for a younger running mate. Harris skillfully kept that door open while pushing both shoulders firmly into the top tier of candidates. Biden, to his credit, also didn't lash out but defended his decades of strong civil rights support. Again, it's nice to see adults running for president.

The reaction to Harris's strong debate has ranged widely. Detractors point to her prosecutor's background as evidence that she's not a true liberal. This misguided purity test assumes that liberals are against the rule of law, which is a false stereotype from dishonest Republicans. Democrats have always believed we are a nation of laws. We just want wise laws that are enforced fairly. These days, Republicans seem only to care about laws that force women to give birth or put immigrant children into cages.

Trump, of course, is the poster child for lawlessness. As a private citizen, he broke laws to satisfy his lust for money and power. He hired untold numbers of undocumented immigrants, skirted regulations, defrauded customers and contractors, and lied about his finances to manipulate the system. As a candidate, he broke campaign finance laws and colluded with foreign adversaries. (Yes, he did. Read the Mueller Report.) As president, he ignores established legal procedures, defies lawful investigations, and obstructs justice (again, read the damned report).

In short, Trump's a crook. Raise your hand if you'd love to see a prosecutor take on Trump in the general election. A criminal president who also happens to be a racist, sexist, regressive, accused rapist, wanna-be dictator deserves to be confronted by a tough prosecutor who also happens to be a liberal, dark-skinned, strong woman.

Harris and Warren already have Republicans panicking. They've redoubled their slurs against Warren, even trying to tie her Native American heritage with claims that she'll pretend to be Black to get "reparation checks." My Republican coworker recently reposed Facebook memes that show Warren with an exaggerated afro hairstyle and feathered headdress. A simple Google image search "meme Warren reparations" shows dozens of disgusting memes that have circulated widely in right-wing social media.

And Harris has recently been attacked as not black enough because her father is Jamaican and her mother is Indian. Even Donald Trump Jr. recently join this racist attack. That race-baiting apple didn't fall far from the father birther tree.

Casual racism against Warren and Harris even sullied the Gazette recently. Columnist Jay Fleitman quipped in his latest piece,

"Or was Warren the one who was bused to white schools and Harris is a Cherokee? I can't keep it straight." Fleitman would surely decry race-baiting attacks on a Republican candidate, but he thinks it's funny regarding Democrats. Trump has given Republicans such as Fleitman permission to flaunt their own racial insensitivity. Is America great again yet?

Despite their early successes, Warren or Harris may not get the nomination. Biden still leads the polls with Bernie Sanders lurking. Buttigieg, Booker, and Castro all had strong debates—although they seem to be running for vice president or 2024.

Trump is beatable, but what's the best approach? Will we need a crusty old white man to thrash a racist old white man? A professor to oust an underachieving rich jerk? A prosecutor to convict a crook? One thing is certain: We'll all need to be grown-ups and vote to send the toddler back to the kids' table where he belongs.

Nationalism, Trumpism, and Patriotism

August 2019

Imagine hearing this during the Red Sox's recent skid out of playoff contention:

"The Red Sox right now are the greatest team in baseball history. You haters are just too blind to see it. You've been brainwashed by the evil sports media making up stuff about them and not reporting their great accomplishments. Their pitching, hitting, and fielding are the best ever, but all you see are side issues that don't matter. The truth is that you don't just hate the Red Sox. You hate baseball! I feel sorry for you."

That sounds silly, doesn't it? I'm a Red Sox fan, but I recognize that this year's team can't seem to pull it together. If I claimed that they're on the verge of repeating as champions, I'd be laughed out of every local sports bar. But here's a verbatim message someone actually sent to me during a recent political discussion:

"Trump right now is the greatest president in American history. You haters are just too blind to see it. You've been brainwashed by the evil news media making up stuff about him and not reporting his great accomplishments. The economy, America's respect in the world, our unity as a nation are the best ever, but all you see are side issues that don't matter. The truth is that you don't just hate Trump. You hate America! I feel sorry for you."

This message is just as silly, considering how divisive and incompetent Trump has been. No major political figure in recent history has been as offensive as Trump, and most of the economic gains that Trump likes to brag about can be traced back to trends stemming from the Obama administration. Yet Trump supporters persist in claiming that Trump is making America great again, and anyone who criticizes him hates America.

Trump's recent tweetstorm urging four first-year members of Congress to "go back" to their original countries instead of "viciously telling the people of the United States ... how our government is to be run" is a clear example of the view that anyone criticizing Trump hates America. Trump ignores the fact that three of these representatives were born in the United States and the fourth has been a citizen longer than Trump's own wife. These four actually are, "the people of the United States" and an integral part of "our government."

When Trump says, "go back," where does he mean? Of course, he wants us to think that these representatives are foreign, but they're not. In reality, they go back to their districts in America, specifically Michigan, Minnesota, New York, and Massachusetts. They won their districts with vote percentages ranging from 78-98 percent. Does Trump hate the Americans in these districts? According to his thinking, yes. By contrast, Trump got barely 46 percent and needed the antiquated and biased Electoral College to bail him out.

Trump, of course, has frequently criticized America, both during his campaign and while in office. His presidential campaign book was called "Crippled America." He has called America "a laughingstock," "foolish," "dumb," "stupid," "weak," "not respected," "going to hell," "a third-world country," and "an embarrassment." How would he respond if the representatives he told to "go back" had attacked America like that?

In fact, he blatantly lies about these representatives, saying one called Americans "garbage" while claiming that another said she loves al Qaeda. Trump loves to criticize what he calls "fake news" from "the enemy of the people," but two minutes of fact-checking shows that Trump is lying. Does someone who lies about Americans hate America?

The shallow idea that criticizing America should be forbidden is called Nationalism. The even shallower idea that criticizing Trump should be forbidden is called Trumpism. These "isms" aren't patriotic. Patriotism is loving America enough to embrace what's great about America while working to ensure safety, opportunity, and justice for all Americans.

The Nationalism-Trumpism combination is dangerous, whether it involves last year's "MAGA Bomber" or the recent El Paso shooter. In fact, the El Paso shooter's written rant includes phrasing remarkably similar to Trump's, especially the term "invasion." Trump often uses that incendiary term on Twitter, in public, and in thousands of Facebook ads. Combining the myth of a flawless president, the scare-tactic of our nation being invaded, and easy access to deadly weapons has led to tragic results. Trump's vacant-eyed teleprompter reading of "hate has no place in America" can't wipe away his countless toxic attacks.

Politics and government are life-and-death issues. In comparison, sports are inconsequential. I wish I could help the Red Sox by stepping to the mound and starting a few games during the stretch run. But I'm fifty-eight years old with a fastball that tops out in the high thirties. Instead, I'll keep rooting for them anyway and, with classic Sox fan hope, wait 'til next year.

And I'm a patriotic American, so I'll keep working to make this country a better place for everyone while looking forward to 2020. A big part of that work will be holding Trump and his Republican enablers accountable when their actions, policies, and values frequently undermine the best qualities of the nation I love.

Signs of Intelligent Life

September 2019

Author's Note: Sometimes fiction can help us see what nonfiction can't. I received more compliments on this column (and less hate mail) than most of my others.

Scientists discovered the technology to observe the alien world so similar to our own back in the 1950s. Communication wasn't possible—only observation. The process was surprisingly simple: applying atomic energy to telescopic lenses and radio waves. Unfortunately, space flight was many decades behind the ability to watch, so meeting these cosmic neighbors wasn't yet possible. Instead, a team of government officials, scientists, philosophers, and educators studied every aspect of the intelligent life on that far-off planet for nearly a century while they simultaneously worked to build a ship to visit the new world.

During those many decades, the observers saw the planet's relatively primitive occupants gradually advance in significant ways, growing technologically, socially, morally, and artistically. Their progress wasn't perfect, and they suffered many setbacks, but they seemed destined to make their world into an advanced society with peace, cooperation, and equal opportunity, given enough time.

But then, just when the observers thought that the alien race might advance enough to make a compatible ally, disaster struck. Frightened and confused by their own progress, they let a leader emerge who represented their worst instincts and preyed upon their weaknesses to lead them down a path of hatred, xenophobia, and deceit. Following his example, the alien creatures eventually descended into bigotry, violence, environmental neglect, and, ultimately, a devastating world war that wiped out all living creatures in less than five years.

This distant tragedy took place only a few years before the observers banded together to complete their great spacecraft for the trip across the gulf of space to the parallel planet. The sad irony was not lost on those who put away childish differences and saw that what united them was far greater than anything that could divide them. They had hoped to come together in peace with the beings on this new world. Sadly, that would never be. As they helplessly watched the other planet destroy itself, they vowed not to let the same fate befall their own existence.

When, at last, their ship landed on the strange planet, two crew members stepped out into the still-smoking remains of the ruined world. This place had once been so lush and full of life, but it was now something from a child's nightmare.

The travelers immediately went to a graveyard where the most intelligent beings on the planet went to die. The first crew member bent down and lifted a long, white bone from the dirt and held it aloft for her companion to see.

"I'm honored to hold what's left of a being so wise and dignified," she said.

"Yes," her crewmate replied. "They were majestic in every way."

The first crewmember held the bone out to the other. "If only these elephants had governed this world," she said with a sigh.

The second crewmember extended one of his three arms and gently lifted the elephant bone from the eight-fingered hand of his crewmate.

"If the elephants had led this world instead of those foolish humans," he mused while examining the bone with five of his seven eyes, "then perhaps there would still be intelligent life here on Earth to greet us."

Impeachment Will Test Us All

October 2019

Beneath the bluster about the current impeachment process is a vital test for this country, specifically for Donald Trump, Democrats, Republicans, the media, and the American public.

Let's start with Trump. Like nearly every other test in his adult life, Trump is failing miserably. He released notes on his call asking the Ukrainian president to investigate Joe Biden, a leading political opponent. These call notes were originally hidden in the administration's most secret server and are basically a confession to an impeachable offense.

Then Trump went on national television and asked China for a similar investigation, doubling-down with a confession to another impeachable offense. He has cynically claimed that he's only interested in rooting out corruption, but when asked if he ever requested that a foreign country investigate corruption involving someone who isn't his political opponent, he evaded the question.

Trump brags about his "perfect" conversation with Ukraine's president while projecting his corruption onto others, calling for the impeachment of Adam Schiff and Nancy Pelosi for overseeing the impeachment inquiry. He even called for Republican Mitt Romney to be impeached for rightly pointing out that Trump's behavior is inappropriate.

And, most troubling, his administration has impeded the investigation by blocking or limiting administration officials from testifying to Congress, both during and before the impeachment inquiry became official. He has also threatened the whistleblower whose complaint revealed Trump's offenses. In short, Trump has committed yet another impeachable offense by obstructing the investigation into his original impeachable offenses.

Trump's earns an impeachment test grade of F-.

How about Democrats? For much of Trump's term, many Democrats wanted party leadership to begin impeachment proceedings. The obvious cases of obstruction of justice outlined in the Mueller Report or Trump's role as an unindicted coconspirator in Michael Cohen's conviction, for example, could have led to impeachment. Speaker Pelosi, in particular, was criticized for slow-walking impeachment. But she predicted two years ago that Trump would "self-impeach," and she has been proven was right. Pelosi waited for Trump to commit specific, obviously impeachable offenses and even provide his own confession.

Pelosi chose House Intelligence Committee Chair Schiff to lead impeachment investigations. With the exception of one slightly misguided parody where he paraphrased Trump's impeachable phone call, Schiff has been relentless and straightforward in his pursuit of justice. And the vast majority of Democrats in the House (some from swing districts that Trump won in 2016), have condemned Trump's actions or endorsed the impeachment inquiry.

The Democrat's grade on the impeachment test so far is a strong A-.

What about Republicans? Most Republicans in Washington have been notably silent on Trump's impeachment-worthy actions. Some are saying Trump was just joking, a defense used for some of his previous offenses. Some have rallied around Trump, claiming that soliciting a foreign government for dirt on a political opponent is, at worst, inappropriate. They've claimed that there was no "quid pro quo" in Trump's phone call. There was quid pro quo, but that's irrelevant to his impeachable offense. Ellen Weintraub, chair of the Federal Elections Commission, put it best: "It is illegal for any person to solicit, accept, or receive anything of value from a foreign national in connection with a U.S. election."

Republicans have proven that they are capable of standing up to Trump on rare occasions. For example, many have objected to his plan to abandon our Kurdish allies to Turkey's dictator. If only Republicans had shown s a fraction of that fortitude in the face of Trump's obviously impeachable behavior. Their grade is a charitable D-.

How is the American media handling this test? Fox News (with some exceptions) and the rest of Trump's right-wing apologists are attacking Biden and the impeachment inquiry. For example, Jay Fleitman's recent Gazette column tried to deflect attention from Trump's corruption by claiming that Democrats are "game-playing" and that the "liberal-leaning media" are ignoring Biden's alleged corruption.

Mainstream media outlets, by contrast, have followed the example of nonpartisan fact-checkers in noting that Trump continues to lie about the impeachment inquiry, and that there is no evidence of

corruption by Biden. In fact, despite right-wing lies, Biden was actually part of official U.S. anti-corruption efforts in Ukraine.

Fox News and the many right-wing Fox imitators have earned a
well-deserved F. Reality-based journalists fare much better with an
A-.

Most importantly, how are we, the American people, doing on
our great national test? Surprisingly well, it turns out. Polling shows
an increase in the percentage of Americans who favor impeachment
since Trump's confession. Currently, more Americans favor the impeachment inquiry than oppose it.

Of course, these impeachment views break along partisan lines,
with Democrats favoring impeachment and Republicans opposing
by wide margins. The ever-elusive "independents" are split on the
subject, as usual. So, at this moment, we Americans have earned an
"incomplete." Once the inquiry is finished and the full evidence
(which seems to get worse for Trump by the minute) comes to light,
let's check back and complete that grade.

Of course, if Trump remains in office, our final exam will be
held in the 2020 voting booth. That exam will have one question:
Which is better for the country, corruption or progress? That should
be the easiest test in American history.

Hoping for Good News Next Fall

November 2019

Once a year for the past fifteen years, always in the stunning peak color of October, I meet with a specialist to monitor an obscure medical issue. I was diagnosed the same year I met my wife, so we've been living with this issue through our whole relationship.

Optimistically speaking, this issue could hibernate within me until I die of old age decades from now. Or it could strike any time, poison my blood, scatter my brain, brittle my bones to chalk. That's the pessimistic possibility.

The specialist always says hello, shakes my hand, asks me how my year has been. He's a friendly man who looks the same now as he did fifteen years ago: short, smart, kind, always half-smiling. I wonder what changes he sees when he looks at me.

"Any shortness of breath?" the specialist asks.

"No," I say.

"Unexplained pains?"

"Just explainable ones," I say. The specialist knows about my bad knees.

"Fatigue a problem?"

"Only when I'm tired."

"Remind me what you do."

"Teacher."

"Oh, yes," the specialist says. "That's great. Married, right?"

"Happily."

"Wonderful. Depression?"

"I'm sad that the president is a hateful criminal." I've made this joke-not-a-joke for three consecutive years.

The specialist chuckles. "You and me, both."

"No depression," I say, smiling.

The specialist asks me to hop up on the examination table. Thanks to a different specialist, my bad knees can still hop when needed. He squeezes my ankles, pokes under my armpits, listens to my heart and lungs.

"Deep breath, please," the specialist says. "Good. Again. Good." Then he scribbles on a lab sheet. "We'll do the usual tests. I'll call tonight."

"Thank you," I say, grateful that this busy and important specialist calls me with lab results the same evening after every yearly visit. So far, he's always had good news.

My wife and I spend the evening keeping busy. We pretend not to worry, talk about anything else, heat leftovers for dinner, watch television nestled with our dog on the couch.

The phone rings around eight. The specialist works late. I answer. He speaks. I nod, thank him, and hang up.

"You're stuck with me for another year," I tell my wife. We sigh, smile, finish our show, walk the dog, talk about plans for the upcoming weekend, go to bed. I have the next morning off work, so I spend a few hours raking those beautiful leaves, grateful that I still can.

What would I have done if the tests had been different? What if the specialist had called with bad news? My wife and I would have finished our show, walked the dog, went to bed. We would have talked about the upcoming weekend—and probably a few more weekends after that. We'd have bigger plans to make.

And the leaves would turn and fall, spectacularly oblivious to our drama.

My wife has her own obscure medical issue and regularly visits her own specialist. Does everyone have a pre-existing condition? Probably.

We're very fortunate to have decent health insurance, which means we don't have to think too much about health insurance, aside from a few forms and phone calls. What if we didn't have health insurance, or if we had bad health insurance? I probably would have never met my specialist. My bad knees would be much worse while raking the leaves.

I'll see my specialist again next year. We'll exchange the same niceties. He'll call me that night with good news. Or he'll tell me that I'll likely die soon without treatments that have unpleasant names, painful side-effects, and reams of insurance forms.

Next fall, we'll also vote for president. The Republican candidate will talk about how he wants everyone to have beautiful health care, but he supports policies that are already taking insurance away from other Americans and degrading the coverage of those still covered.

The Democrat might be someone who supports Medicare for All, or Medicare for more than have it now, or expanding Obamacare with a public option. We'll have primaries soon to help make that choice. Some people will be mad about the result, just as they were in 2016. No offense, but tough noogies. Mad or not, we all need to vote this time. No excuses.

Whatever health plan emerges from the Democratic primary will improve what the country does now and be light years better than anything Republicans have to offer. Well, better for human beings, anyway. The Republican plan will benefit corporations that treat illness and death as profit centers. Not voting because the Democratic nominee's health plan isn't perfect would be like wishing for the whole country to get bad test results.

Deep-red Kentucky recently elected a Democratic governor in large part because he supported the Obamacare Medicaid expansion. Kentuckians did the right thing. Surely the rest of us can as well. I long for a double-dose of good news next fall: one from my specialist and another from the election. I want everyone to have health care that actually cares for health instead of bringing dread about lack of coverage.

Those leaves will keep turning. I'd like us all to be around to enjoy them for many autumns to come.

Not This Time

December 2019

I chased down the long rebound at the top of the key and faced the basket. Chris, the best player in the gym, took up his defensive position. I faked right and dribbled left, creating just enough space to rise up with a left-handed floater. The ball inched above Chris's block attempt, kissed high off the backboard, and slipped through the net.

Game point. Chris turned to me and said, "Nice shot!"

That was more than a decade ago, just before age and injuries forced me to quit pick-up basketball. You probably don't remember my big retirement ceremony on ESPN because there wasn't one.

I saw Chris at the gym the other day. He doesn't play any longer either, but that's a bigger loss than my retirement. Chris was on another level. I spent most games chasing him while he mixed deep jumpers with driving layups. He got the better of me about ninety percent of the time. That game-winning floater was the best of my treasured ten percent.

We chatted briefly on the way to the exercise bikes and rowing machines. It turns out that Chris enjoys my columns, which is always nice to hear.

"I wish I had your optimism," he said. "I'm worried that we're stuck with this guy for another term."

I can't blame Chris for thinking "this guy" might get re-elected—even with an abysmal approval rating, pervasive incompetence, and impeachable crimes. Trump defied the odds once, so it's possible he could do it again.

As Chris and I talked, I counted off the crazy circumstances that aligned for Trump in 2016. He had the Electoral College, that outdated affirmative action program for less qualified Republican presidential candidates. But Trump's state-by-state approval is currently underwater in the several swing states where he squeaked by in 2016. And he's struggling in some red states that he needs for any chance at re-election.

What about the fake 2016 scandals like Hillary's emails? Well, Trump's getting impeached for trying to get Ukraine to fake-investigate Democrats, so he's clearly trying to cheat again. But the 2020 nominee won't be the target of three decades of conspiracies, as Hillary was. Will Russia hack and Wikileaks dump? Probably, but that won't fool as many gullible people as in 2016. The mainstream media covered every Trump lie as if it were legitimate back then. But now, CNN and others have discovered that fact-checking makes for excellent journalism and still generates ratings.

Will Bernie-or-Busters stay home, vote third-party, or write in Bernie's name? Possibly. But there seem to be fewer of them now, and some have probably learned the harsh lesson that not voting for the Democratic nominee is almost as bad as voting for Trump.

Will there be people in MAGA hats who say, "I don't know much about Trump, but he seems like a successful businessman who can drain the swamp and help the little guy while behaving more presidential once he's in office"? Sadly, more than a few. But not as many as in 2016. That level of ignorance is hard to maintain in the face of non-stop infantile behavior, pervasive dishonesty, tax breaks for the rich, mounting deficits, and widespread corruption. "Fool me once," as the saying goes.

Most important, will Americans be as apathetic as they were in 2016? Will anyone say, "I'm not going to bother voting because Trump has no chance"? That would be the dumbest move of all. We learned in 2016 that even when a candidate has a ninety percent chance to win, ten percent can still happen.

Elections since 2016 certainly show that voters don't want Trump or the Republicans who have hitched their broken wagons to his burned-out star. Despite Gerrymandered districts and voter suppression efforts, Democrats have been winning in previously red areas throughout Trump's term.

Most notably, the Democrat's 2018 victory in the House paved the way for impeachment proceedings. Republicans in the Senate will probably thwart Trump's expulsion, but his high crimes and misdemeanors will be on full display. Will a significant percentage of Americans vote for a criminal in 2020? Yes, absolutely. Will that percentage be enough for a second term? Realistically and optimistically, no.

"I hope you're right," Chris said. Me too.

It was time for Chris and me to start our respective low-impact workouts. I didn't ask him, "Hey, remember when I hit the game-winning shot over you?" I'm sure he doesn't. When he relives his playing days, he probably remembers making better plays against players far better than I am.

I still recall his words, "Nice shot!" That was classy. He recognized that I beat him fair and square. He didn't begrudge my ten percent edging out his ninety. He knew I didn't cheat. I didn't goad the mainstream media to scream in Chris's face about Hillary's server while he tried to guard me. Fox News didn't set illegal screens, and Russia didn't knee him in the groin.

Trump could still win in 2020, of course. If he earns it fair and square, we'll keep fighting for the next elections, local, state, and federal. But Trump's already trying to cheat again because that's his only path to victory. We can't let him get away with it this time.

Case Study #45: The Neighborhood v. Donald J. Smith

January 2020

Background: Donald J. Smith moved to the Presidential Heights neighborhood four years ago and immediately started campaigning for president of the Neighborhood Board. Smith, who had no municipal government experience, claimed to be an extremely successful entrepreneur, despite several very public bankruptcies. He remained secretive about the sources of his wealth (beyond inheritance).

Smith's election slogan, "Make the Neighborhood Great Again," offended many residents who thought their neighborhood was already great. Smith's platform had few policies but many accusations that other neighborhoods were dangerous. He threatened to ban neighborhood visitors based on their religion and proposed building a wall around the neighborhood and somehow making the residents on the other side pay for it. He immediately gained an almost cultish following among some community members for his fancy mansion, flashy cars, and brash, "speaks-his-mind" ways.

Other community members were skeptical, finding Smith rude, incompetent, and corrupt. They contacted residents of Smith's previous neighborhoods and learned about his questionable past, including constant litigation and law enforcement scrapes. Smith called these reports "fake news" meant to distract from the corruption of his election opponent, a longtime resident and active board member. Despite no evidence for these accusations, Smith's supporters believed him.

After all the votes were counted, Smith was significantly behind, but he won because an obscure bylaw gave more votes to households with greater square footage. During Smith's subsequent three years as board president, a majority of his neighbors disapproved of his incompetent leadership and frequent embarrassing incidents. Still, a vocal minority continued their support, and some even called him the best president ever.

Case Notes: The board recently voted to continue the neighborhood's annual donation to a local food bank. Smith's job was to make sure the funds were sent and to host a public meeting with the food bank director to promote the charity.

Then the local Sheriff's office received an anonymous tip that Smith hadn't forwarded the donation and wasn't scheduling the public meeting. The tipster claimed that Smith had sent his assistants to the food bank to investigate the leading candidate to replace Smith as board president, a former board member whose family had some dealings with the food bank in the past. The Sheriff had gone out of his way to bury several previous complaints against Smith, raising serious concerns when the Sheriff also failed to investigate the anonymous tip.

Smith himself released notes of a call with the food bank director, describing the call as, "perfect." But the notes showed that Smith asked directly for a "favor" when the head of the food bank asked about the neighborhood's donation. The call notes amounted to a confession that Smith had withheld the donation for his own benefit, but he continued to claim that he had done nothing wrong. Smith's supporters urged their neighbors to read the call notes. But most of Smith's supporters hadn't actually read those notes or they would have realized that their leader had incriminated himself.

Meanwhile, the local state police began investigating because the Sheriff wouldn't. Although the state police were acting within their jurisdiction, Smith refused to cooperate. He ordered board members with direct knowledge of the events not to testify and hid documents required by board bylaws. The police held public hearings where some witnesses braved threats from Smith to testify that Smith had abused his position to extract political favors from the food bank. Despite Smith's stonewalling, the police discovered that Smith had committed multiple crimes relating to withholding the donation and hindering investigators.

Smith himself even said publicly that other charities should investigate his election opponent. One of Smith's top assistants said that Smith does these kinds of things, "all the time," and anyone concerned about this corruption should, "get over it." Smith and his supporters attacked the anonymous tipster and the state police as the real criminals. When the local papers covered the investigation, Smith smeared them as, "enemies of the neighborhood."

After the state police investigation, the board voted to have a formal proceeding to consider removing Smith from the board presidency. According to the board bylaws, a committee currently controlled by Smith's supporters was charged with this proceeding. The bylaws called for this review committee to be impartial, but

Smith's supporters on the committee bragged that they would dismiss the proceedings in Smith's favor, not even bothering to pretend that they would be fair.

Discussion Questions: (1) Should Smith's troubling past influence how members of his neighborhood view his current behavior? (2) How should the board deal with Smith's flagrant violations of board policies? (3) How should residents deal with the review committee members who reject their duty to be impartial jurors? (4) How should residents react to Smith's attacks on the investigators and the press? (5) Should Smith be removed from office? (6) Should Smith face criminal charges for his actions? (7) What would happen if Smith had committed these crimes in a powerful position more important than a local board—President of the United States, for example? (8) Why did anyone vote for Donald J. Smith in the first place, and how could anyone consider reelecting him after his obvious abuse of power?

Please discuss.

What Kind of Criminal is Donald Trump?

February 2020

Some folks might read the title of this column and think, "Wait a minute. Trump isn't a criminal." Bless their hearts. They should take a deep breath and lie down. Citizenship requires that we stand up for the truth.

What are Trump's crimes? Here's a partial list, all well documented in the reality-based free press:

He illegally discriminated against prospective Black and Hispanic tenants in his real estate business way back in the 1970s. He avoided charges by settling with the Justice Department and paying a fine.

He illegally hired undocumented workers for his various businesses. He avoided charges by using his money and influence to sweep those crimes under the rug.

He illegally operated a fraudulent "university" and a self-dealing "foundation." He avoided charges by paying millions of dollars to settle those cases.

He has been credibly accused of sexual harassment/assault by more than a dozen women. He avoided charges by attacking his victims and spending untold fortunes on legal defense.

He was an unindicted co-conspirator in the illegal porn-star adultery payoffs that landed his personal lawyer in prison. He avoided charges largely because of a questionable Justice Department guideline that says sitting presidents can't be indicted.

He illegally obstructed justice in the investigation of his 2016 election collusion with Russia. He avoided charges because Special Counsel Robert Mueller declined to make a recommendation about whether or not his actions were criminal. Spoiler alert: Thousands of former federal prosecutors say his actions were, indeed, criminal.

He illegally solicited election interference from a foreign nation, illegally obstructed the Congressional investigation of his actions, illegally extorted/bribed a foreign leader for political favors, and illegally withheld foreign aid approved by Congress. He avoided charges because he's a sitting president. He was impeached but not removed from office because Republicans in the Senate served as his tainted jury and bent reality to suit their political motives.

So, yes, Donald Trump is a criminal. Anyone who thinks that Trump's crimes haven't been proven should get a change-of-address form and use indelible ink to indicate a new home planet. Seriously. Accepting basic reality should be a condition of residing on Earth, and being able to identify an obviously criminal president should be a requirement for American citizenship.

What kind of criminal is Donald Trump? Sociologist Paul Kooistra, in his excellent book, "Criminals as Heroes," explores the concept of the "Robin Hood Criminal," a law-breaking hero who arises, "when large numbers of people become disenchanted with the quality of justice represented by law and politics." (Full disclosure: Kooistra is my friend and brother-in-law, married to my wife's sister. He's also a terrific tennis player and a damned fine sociologist.)

Republicans have spent decades trying to convince Americans that government is the enemy. In such an environment, it's easy to see how Trump's claims of championing "the forgotten man" and "draining the swamp" could be superficially appealing.

But, as Kooistra notes, "the actual deeds and characteristics of heroic criminals played only a minor part in elevating them to such lofty status. A good public relations man and a receptive audience may be far more important." Trump's "actual deeds and characteristics" are the antithesis of basic American values. His big legislative efforts, for example, have been terrible for all but the wealthy. He weakened the Affordable Care Act, leading to a rise in the uninsured rate. And his absurd tax cut was a boon to the ultra-rich and corporations but left the "forgotten man," well, largely forgotten.

And Trump is obviously his loudest "public relations man." That quality has been described as his "genius" over the years because he has bragged, blustered, and bloviated his way to avoid consequences for his crimes while fooling millions of people into believing that he's on their side. This fake "Criminal Hero" has swindled his way to the White House by pretending not to be a criminal and wearing his rumpled suit as a very thinly veiled hero costume.

Trump's worst wrath goes to the public servants who reveal his true criminality. He hates Robert Mueller, Nancy Pelosi, Adam Schiff, Jerry Nadler, et. al, for the same reasons all criminals hate cops. Cops strive to keep criminals from getting away with their crimes. Conversely, Trump loves his right-wing media defenders, his misleading lawyers, and his enablers in Congress because they're his accomplices. That's also why he loves his voters, which is deeply sad, considering how his policies hurt his supporters at least as much as his detractors.

The question, "What kind of criminal is Donald Trump?" has a clear answer. He's a con artist, huckster, and fraud. He'll never take responsibility for his crimes because he seems to have fooled even himself into believing that he's a hero. In the coming months, we'll see further evidence of his crimes, but the people confused enough to think he's a hero won't care.

Ultimately, the result of Trump's impeachment trial is temporary. Another fake criminal hero, O.J. Simpson, won his first trial too—but not his second. Trump's second trial will be the election, and "We the People," not the sycophantic Republican-led Senate, will be his jury. Let's use our vote to make sure Trump answers for his crimes.

Heads Up for the Wrecking Ball

March 2020

I'm not a hater or a pawn of the establishment. But, with all due respect, I'm worried about Bernie Sanders as the potential Democratic nominee for president. I'll fight for Sanders if he's the nominee because he's far better than Trump, but I have two major concerns right now. First, Elizabeth Warren is better. Second, Republicans can't wait to attack Sanders.

Warren is a classic "happy warrior," the toughest and most likable candidate in the race. She could decimate Trump in a debate, sprint into the crowd, and take hundreds of smiling selfies with the audience. And she was a Republican until she saw how Republicans were failing everyday Americans, so she can appeal to disenchanted Republicans who might still be open-minded.

She's also the most prepared to be an effective president, considering her excellence at the highest levels of education, the private sector, and government. Her Consumer Financial Protection Bureau has helped millions of people recover billions of dollars from manipulative corporations. She has real accomplishments, well-articulated proposals, and practical plans.

As for potential Republican attacks on Sanders, here's the question I ask when someone tells me that Sanders would have beaten Trump in 2016: What's the worst thing Hillary Clinton said about Sanders during their campaign? People usually respond, "I don't know." Sometimes they say, "She called him unqualified." I remind them that was a misquote.

In fact, Clinton soundly defeated Sanders without needing to attack and embarrass a long-term ally. Will Trump and the Republicans treat Sanders as well? Not a chance. I'm not attacking Sanders, but Trump will. Sanders polls well against Trump now partly because he hasn't faced sustained attacks the likes of which Trump and the Republicans will launch.

Republicans are terrible at governing, but they know how to swing a wrecking ball. They'll find plenty about Sanders to bash and smash just by Googling his public record. Most prominently, Sanders calls himself a Democratic Socialist, and a recent Gallup poll showed that a majority of Americans wouldn't vote for a Socialist.

It's not rocket surgery to understand that many Americans put "Socialism" in scare-quotes. I grew up in rural Pennsylvania where most people think Socialism is Communism on dictatorial steroids. Many believe Sanders is the same kind of Socialist that Hitler was. Yes, that's ridiculous, but people believe ridiculous things. And Sanders has spoken favorably about the Sandinistas and Fidel Castro, which many pundits say will cost him Florida's electoral votes. Lose Pennsylvania and Florida, and the election is over.

Sanders is vulnerable to plenty of other attacks. He doesn't explain his health care and tax plans well enough to keep Republicans from grossly misrepresenting them. He's also problematic on gun issues. Republicans are far worse, but that won't stop Trump from lying to spin the issue against Sanders. And Trump will claim that Sanders is a career politician, a member of the do-nothing "establishment," a rich guy pretending to be a revolutionary.

Sanders frequently criticizes the Democratic Party, so it's hard to see him helping with crucial Congressional races or choosing a unifying person as his running mate. Trump will even claim that Sanders was mean to Hillary and try to rewrite history with Sanders as the villain of 2016 instead of himself.

Then add obvious attacks on Sanders's health and age. And in response to Trump's sexist history, Republicans will cloud the issue by pulling out decades-old writings by Sanders about women having rape fantasies and getting cancer from sexual repression. Or they'll point out that Sanders had a child out of wedlock who was on welfare. Trump will rant that Sanders has a terrible employment history in contrast to his false claims of business success.

Republicans will quote the many people who say Sanders is hard to work with and has a terrible temper. That's partly a projection of Trump's flaws, but there's just enough truth to make it stick. Trump will claim that Sanders enables his "Bernie Bro" bullies even though MAGA rallies resemble extended versions of George Orwell's "Two Minutes Hate."

Sanders voted for the 1994 Crime Bill and against Amber Alerts while Trump will falsely boast about reforming criminal justice. Trump has already claimed that Russia controls Sanders, which is like the pot calling the kettle a kitchen implement. Sanders pushed for dumping Vermont's nuclear waste in rural Texas, which Trump will hypocritically use to claim Sanders is bad for the environment and Hispanic Americans. Republicans will even twist Sanders's occasional criticisms of Obama to paint him as a racist.

And Republicans will trot out attacks we can't yet imagine. Many will be lies, but Trump is proof that voters believe obvious lies. With each new and recycled attack, Trump will chip away support for Sanders. And very few people who don't already support Sanders will believe his rebuttals.

Again, I can't emphasize enough that I'll support Sanders if he's the nominee. I hope I'm wrong about these concerns. But we need to vet him more thoroughly now so that he can build defenses against inevitable Republican attacks—or so that we can choose a better candidate. Trump got elected partly because people believed his attacks on Clinton. We can't let that happen to Sanders or anyone else.

Dispatches From Coronaville

April 2020

One month ago, I was writing about the presidential primary. That seems so long ago. The world has turned upside-down since then. We're now fully immersed in the alternative universe that began on November 8, 2016, with the election of a reality TV host who bankrupts casinos, brags about sexual assault, and is clueless in the face of a national emergency.

Not much makes sense during this Trumpandemic. I teach my now-all-online classes most of the day, occasionally peeking at reports on the insanity surrounding us. I post funny photos of my dog with encouraging words on Facebook and help my wife make face-masks. I wore one of those homemade masks to the post office to ship some excess toilet paper across the country to loved ones. No one could tell if I was smiling or silently screaming behind that mask. I was smiling, but one sniffling guy with no mask standing too close might have nudged me into a scream. Does anyone else feel like you're sometimes holding yourself together with broken clothes pins and rusty twist-ties? You're not alone.

I admire writers who can conjure a coherent essay right now. I can't. Not this month, at least. Maybe in May. Doesn't May sound nice? Far away, but you can almost see it if you squint. For now, the best I can do is "Dispatches from Coronaville," some unconnected observations that provide brief glimpses of something adjacent to clarity.

Dispatch #1: Here's a public service announcement for everyone working from home these days. When doing a video conference, park your laptop or monitor atop a shoebox to elevate it. No matter how attractive we might be, we all look like gargoyles when we loom over our webcam. Nobody wants to see us like that.

Dispatch #2: Remember when Trump was talking about "opening up the country" as soon as possible? He probably meant that when the unemployment rate and the stock market surge in opposite directions, his reelected gets flushed. So he blathered about easing restrictions. It seems so long ago, but that was March 24.

The most absurd part of Trump's strategy was his desire to "pack the churches" on Easter. News flash: Packing any space with human germ delivery systems during a pandemic is stupid and dangerous. Imagine Fox News or Rush Limbaugh reacting if Barack Obama had suggested "packing the churches" during a virus outbreak. They would have screamed that Obama wanted to mass murder every Christian in America. Of course, Obama wasn't insane enough to suggest anything so dumb. But for Trump, that was just a tiny sapling in his idiocy forest.

An actual medical expert, Dr. Anthony Fauci (the poor soul who often has to stand dangerously close to Trump at those mind-numbing daily briefings), said Trump's "pack the churches" plan was, "an aspirational projection to give people some hope." That's code for calling Trump a delusional liar while keeping your job trying to prevent the toddler president from killing millions of people.

Dispatch #3: My fellow *Daily Hampshire Gazette* columnist Jay Fleitman recently wrote that we shouldn't watch news coverage of the pandemic because it's "melodramatic bordering on hysterical," and medical experts on the news "seem overwrought" and will make viewers "unnecessarily anxious." Oh, those awful news people causing anxiety during a pandemic! Fleitman suggested we watch the daily briefing with Fauci and Dr. Deborah Brix instead of the news.

Fleitman should trade his column for a hobby more suited to his talent: magic. He made Trump and his misinformation, insults, lies, and general foolishness at the daily briefings completely disappear! Presto! Gosh, we wouldn't want those "hysterical, overwrought" medical experts on the news getting people "unnecessarily anxious" when we have the least qualified president in history to spout complete nonsense while Fauci and Brix visibly wince.

Dispatch #4: Hey, did you hear? The pandemic's a hoax! A diehard Trump worshipper told me that he knows the "Demoncrats" and the "Commie Media" are exaggerating COVID-19 to make Trump look bad. He claimed that the disease has actually been around for decades. He read it on his favorite website, so it must be true. I guess he doesn't know that the "19" stands for the year 2019. When. The. First. Cases. Appeared. Oh. My. God.

Dispatch #5: Let's finish with something positive to counteract the specter of Trump looming over our alternate universe lives.

Recently, our beloved neighbors needed some legal papers witnessed. So we set up a table in our driveway on a beautiful weekday morning. Our friends walked over and signed their papers at the driveway table while we watched from our porch. Then they backed up to keep a proper distance while we came out and signed as witnesses. Then we backed off while they collected the papers. We chatted a while, happy for in-person conversation. Finally, we all waved goodbye, called out words of encouragement, and went inside to wash our hands and return to our various remote jobs.

Neighborly interactions may have changed, but we citizens of Coronaville can still be there for each other. The same truth that guided us before we entered this alternate universe is even more important now: We're all in this together—just, you know, from at least six feet apart.

Welcome to the "Fever Cabin"

May 2020

Author's Note: This essay became the "Author's Afterword" for Fever Cabin, *the novella I wrote during the early weeks of the pandemic lockdown.*

On Thursday, March 12, 2020, as I drove home from work, I wondered what it would be like to keep driving. We had learned that day that our campus would be closing for the next three weeks, possibly longer. I imagined heading for an isolated cabin and hunkering down to ride out the pandemic that was washing across the country. What would it be like to cut myself off from family, home, work, news—from the whole world?

I thought about what I would do if I had been infected with COVID-19. I usually don't entertain worst-case scenarios, but I indulged the prospect as I navigated the route I had driven thousands of times before. What if I had shaken one too many student hands during the last few days? What if I had hugged one too many colleagues after we talked about the deadly plague that dominated hallway and office conversations? What if I brought the virus home with me and infected my wife?

Could I isolate myself from everything that had seemed important in my life up to that point?

Of course not. My wife and family are the greatest sources of love and belonging in my life. My work helps me afford my home and, more importantly, lets me contribute to making the lives around me better. Keeping informed helps me contribute as a knowledgeable citizen in a complex world. I could never leave these beloved aspects of my life behind.

But the classic fiction writer's question ("What if?") still tickled my imagination as I drove home. I wouldn't keep driving until I disappeared, but what if I made up someone who did?

I pondered that fictional man who ran away. Who would he be? What if he had good reasons to suspect that he'd been infected? What if he had been exposed to the disease in a way that he didn't want to explain to his family? What if he had the means and the motive to step outside his life? What kind of person could do this? He'd be cynical in a time desperate for hope, superficial when he needed depth, complacent when called to meaningful action, successful but overflowing with doubt.

While I definitely didn't want to be that man, I kept thinking about him. When I got off the interstate, I parked on a side street, grabbed a notebook, and jotted these words: "Guy possibly infected by coworker. Isolates in cabin for two weeks. Keeps journal." I stuck the note in my pocket, drove the last few miles home, embraced my wife, checked the news, and started planning how to move my on-campus classes online.

The next day, I spent forty-five minutes isolating myself in the basement on the exercise bike where I have a stand for my laptop so that I can write while I pedal. That's kept me motivated for writing and exercising. On that first day, I wrote the initial journal entry for my fictional protagonist in his isolation cabin. The writing process was intriguing and kept my mind moving creatively during a crazy time when writing coherent nonfiction (sometimes even functioning coherently) was difficult. Tapping out a few hundred speculative words while spinning in place felt like an anchor holding me steady in the pandemic storm.

The next day, I reread my previous day's writing while taking short breaks from working on my classes and communicating with students and colleagues. Then I guessed what my character's second journal entry might be, climbed aboard the exercise bike, and wrote a few hundred more words.

Then, as we have all tried to do during this pandemic, I kept going.

For the next month, I drafted new journal days while sweating in the basement. My protagonist developed a family, a career, a point of view, a past, and even an inkling of his future. I shared the idea with a few friends who wanted to read the finished story. When it became long enough to be a short book, I thought I might try to publish it and donate any profits to organizations helping people during the pandemic.

The completed manuscript was different from anything that I'd ever written, and I had no idea if it was any good. The title was the only part that I knew was terrific: "Fever Cabin." So I sent the manuscript to some writers I trusted and asked if they would "blurb" it— meaning write a brief comment about the book. To my surprise, they wrote back quickly with encouragement and praise way beyond what I expected.

What started as the flight of my anxious imagination during a pivotal drive home is now an actual book. Anyone who buys "Fever Cabin" will be donating to The Community Foundation of Western Massachusetts COVID-19 Response Fund (to help people right here where we live) and Feed America (to provide food assistance for people across the country).

As a bonus for your donation, you'll get an odd story that I hope you'll appreciate during these more-than-odd times, maybe some reading material to help you get through another day of isolation in your own fever cabin. And you'll have my gratitude for your contribution.

Vote-By-Mail Reflects the Best of America

June 2020

Forty-five years ago, my junior high class visited our local post office in Hyndman, Pennsylvania. The postmaster, Harry T. "Henskie" Ritchey, taught us the newfangled, five-digit zip codes and two-letter state abbreviations that were slowly catching on after more than a decade of use.

Mr. Ritchey spoke reverently about working for the USA and about how the Post Office was in our Constitution. He had been Postmaster for nearly thirty years by that point, since just after WWII when the Post Office led the country by hiring many minorities and women, helping lay the groundwork for the Civil Rights and Women's Rights movements.

Mr. Ritchey also asked what we thought of the price of a first-class stamp, which had just risen from eight to ten cents. Back then, a dime could buy a bag of candy or a packet of baseball cards, so I said, "Ten cents seems like a lot."

"Think about it," Mr. Ritchey replied. "How much would you charge to take a letter from your house to a friend who lives in Maryland?" Maryland was close but still a serious trip for a kid my age. "What about a cousin in Florida? Or California?" he asked, naming far-away places I could barely imagine. "What if you had only a few days to deliver that letter and thousands more? Does ten cents still seem too much?"

"I guess not," I marveled.

These days, I marvel in a different way when I browse social media. Donald Trump recently tweeted, "The United States cannot have all Mail In Ballots. It will be the greatest Rigged Election in history." He ranted in another tweet, "There is NO WAY (ZERO!) that Mail-In Ballots will be anything less than substantially fraudulent."

Trump's insulting lies about voting and the Post Office are so egregious that Twitter fact-checked him, linking to evidence that voting by mail is not prone to fraud. Twitter's fact-check is a good start. The Brennen Center for Justice ("The False Narrative of Vote-by-Mail Fraud") and FactCheck.org ("More False Mail-In Ballot Claims from Trump") have also done great work debunking lies about mail-in voting.

On Facebook, I found people mimicking Trump's foolishness with posts like this: "We the People say no to vote-by-mail fraud!" Actually, nearly every poll shows strong majorities of "We the People" support voting by mail. Another post claimed that "We stand in line at Target, Walmart, Lowe's, etc. We can stand in line in November. Say no to mail-in voting!" This is pure nonsense.

Every citizen should have the opportunity to vote safely and securely. Lines at retailers have nothing to do with voting. But if people insist on comparing shopping and voting, this makes more sense: "If we can get products from Target, Walmart, and Lowe's by mail, then we can vote by mail!"

Americans trust the postal service with far more than just their shopping. We send our saliva DNA through the mail when we do those Ancestry or 23andMe genetic tests. Men put their semen in the mail to send it off for sperm-count testing. Lots of folks even mail out our own fecal matter for colon cancer screenings. If the postal service is good enough to keep our precious bodily fluids secure, then it's good enough for our votes as well.

No American should have to stand in long lines to exercise the constitutional right to vote, especially with a pandemic in progress. Several states have been voting by mail for years without problems. My friends and family members in Colorado, for example, vote by mail. Their votes aren't fraudulent.

Our military members have been voting by mail from deployments away from home since the Civil War. Our troops' votes aren't fraudulent. Millions of people vote absentee by mail, and their votes aren't fraudulent. Trump himself voted by mail while president, and two of his primary spokespeople, Kellyanne Conway and Kayleigh McEnany, have both voted by mail in the past—yet they repeat Trump's lies. Trump and his minions might be frauds, but their votes-by-mail are legitimate.

The Post Office makes voting easier for all Americans, especially those who live in densely populated cities and whose voting has been systematically suppressed for decades by poor transportation infrastructure, long lines, and limited polling places and voting machines. It's no coincidence that Trump doesn't want to promote voting by the Americans who have recently been demonstrating against racism. Just as Trump recently gassed peaceful protestors outside the White House for a ridiculous photo op, he also attacks voting-by-mail to limit the voices of Americans he sees as an obstacle to his authoritarianism.

When Congressional Democrats proposed expanding mail-in voting for the upcoming election, Trump said that would mean "you'd never have a Republican elected in this country again"—although research shows that voting-by-mail doesn't disproportionately benefit either party. He even said in 2016, "If you're not going to vote for me, do not vote." That's how a tin-pot dictator talks. Trump keeps frothing about a "rigged election" because he wants an excuse for losing in November. No president has ever so deeply misunderstood basic American values related to elections.

Two years ago, Henskie Ritchey died on his 101st birthday. I share his reverence for the Post Office, especially how that great institution can promote equal voting with safety and security during this time of pandemic and unrest. Massachusetts will allow mail-in absentee ballots for anyone concerned about in-person voting during the pandemic.

That's how I plan to vote for Joe Biden, a candidate who supports mail-in voting and who is far more qualified to deal with pandemics and racial injustice (and everything else) than the current, temporary occupant of the bunker beneath the White House.

We're Home

July 2020

While pedaling my bike through a nearby neighborhood, I saw a homemade sign someone had set up at an intersection. A wooden post held eight vibrantly painted boards pointing like arrows in various directions, each board displaying the word "home."

I parked and observed the sign from every angle, struck by its powerful message: Home is everywhere. No matter what direction we travel, literally or metaphorically, we're close to home.

During this pandemic, "home" feels even more welcoming than usual. Our home is a safe place, away from the relentless virus. The threat of infection has been climbing in places where people left their homes too quickly for risky interactions at parties, restaurants, bars—even idiotic political rallies.

The security of home assumes access to a welcoming place. How many people aren't safe at home because of abuse, neglect, or rejection? Even one is too many. And a safe home implies any home at all. Homelessness, especially during a pandemic, might be the most dangerous and difficult life a person can live.

Then I noticed that the top arrow of the sign was different. Showing two words that I spoke aloud: "Go home." Those words sounded like an imperative, even a command. And they sounded sadly familiar. For generations, women in the workplace were told to "go home." Some still are. Many immigrants have been hearing "go home" since the beginning of our nation. Refugees fleeing violence and persecution are met today at our border with official orders to "go home." Those orders mock the welcome embodied by the Statue of Liberty: "Give me your tired, your poor ..."

"Go home" sounds strikingly like Donald Trump's words to four minority women members of Congress whose main offenses seemed to be varying shades of brown skin and calling out Trump's rejection of core American values. "Go back" the president tweeted, even though three of the four were born in this country, and the fourth has been a citizen longer than Trump's current wife.

"Go home" has been shouted at countless anti-racism protestors during recent weeks, despite the fact that these protestors often march in their own neighborhoods. Telling them to "go home" says that their presence is unwelcome, their voices should be silent, their lives don't matter.

Trump recently said that the anti-racist Black Lives Matter movement is a "symbol of hate." Then he claimed that memorials to treasonous racists represent the "history, heritage, and greatness of our country." And when Trump was asked about his message to Black Americans, he replied, "If you don't understand your history, you will go back to it again." Rather than making America great again, "go home" for Trump seems to be a callback to the racist values of the Confederacy. A phrase as short as "Go home" (or "go back") can carry an entire encyclopedia of bigotry.

But the longer I looked at the simple sculpture of wood, nails, and paint, the more I realized that the word "home" outnumbered the phrase "go home" seven to one. My initial positive impression returned even stronger than before. "Go home" was soon drowned out by "home, home, home, home, home, home, and home," over and over, rolling through my mind as the words climbed the rungs of the sign, growing in strength, rising to a crescendo.

A pandemic makes for a bad time to knock on doors, so I didn't find out who made the sign. But I want to thank the artist for providing inspiration. As I biked the few miles back to the house that I call home, the concluding words of our national anthem echoed in my thoughts. This country is the "home of the brave," not the home of cowards who reject anyone outside a narrow definition of what it means to be an American or a life that matters.

The cacophony of bigotry and oppression from Trump and his enablers is no match for the song of inclusion rising from protests around the country. For every narrow-minded shout of "Go home!" we have a seven-fold choir singing, "We are home!"

Our neighborhood is our home. Our state is our home. Our country is our home. Our world is our home. Home is a place for all who want to work together to form a more perfect union. With our voices, our marches, and our votes, in every direction across the land, let's build the best home we can.

Considering Joe Biden's Brain

August 2020

Jay Fleitman's most recent *Gazette* column calls into question Joe Biden's cognitive abilities. I read Fleitman's column closely and gave it serious consideration, and, I must confess, I'm concerned. The column has identified someone who lacks the critical thinking skills to be taken seriously.

Joe Biden? No, he's just fine. I'm worried about Jay Fleitman.

Let's disregard that Fleitman (a pulmonologist) is making a neurological diagnosis. Let's also set aside the issue of a physician rendering that diagnosis without examining the subject, especially such a damning diagnosis: "[Biden] clearly has a degenerative neurological disorder in which dementia is a part." Presumably, the medical profession has appropriate ethical guidelines for these situations.

I won't pretend to be a physician. I'm an English teacher, so I'll assess the cognitive skills Fleitman shows in writing his attack on Biden.

Usually, Fleitman's columns are simply annoying and not worth evaluating. But Trump's enablers have made Biden's cognitive ability a central thrust of their flailing campaign. They know that Trump can't win on the issues or his record, and they're desperately projecting Trump's obvious flaws onto Biden. So it's worth debunking these attacks, especially when presented with faux medical authority.

Fleitman bases much of his attack on three Biden videos that he says are "signs of significant cognitive defects." But the real defects are Fleitman's misrepresentations of these videos.

One clip shows Biden saying this about his experience with nurses: "They'd actually breathe in my nostrils to make me move, to get me moving." That may sound strange, but Fleitman goes on to mischaracterize Biden's comment.

Fleitman wrote that Biden said the nurse "whispered in his ear that if anything medically serious would happen to him, that she could breathe up through his nose and bring him back to health." That's not remotely what Biden said. Frankly, Fleitman's dishonest misquote of Biden is more concerning than Biden's oddly vivid anecdote.

The second video shows Biden starting a speech with a somewhat ineffective joke about local landmarks to appeal to his audience in Wilmington, Delaware, Biden's home state. Biden acknowledges the failed joke, laughs it off, and goes on to talk in detail about the location. Then he presents a coherent, animated, insightful, hour-long campaign speech.

Fleitman didn't get the joke because he's not from Wilmington. Neither am I, but I found the full video of Biden's speech, watched it, and understood the context. Why didn't Fleitman do the same before falsely claiming that Biden "clearly did not know where he was"? Biden obviously knows where he is. Does Fleitman know where the search box on his internet browser is?

Fleitman's third video is, again, cherry-picked from a longer source. Minimal research shows the full video of Biden saying "2020" when he meant "2000." Fleitman says this simple mistake shows cognitive decline. But Fleitman himself wrote in his column that Biden said "two or three years ago" when Biden actually said, "two censuses ago." That's also a simple mistake that shows Fleitman can't even pass the cognitive test he applies to Biden.

Later in his column, Fleitman claims that Biden said 120 million Americans had died of COVID, which would be an obvious error. But the error (lie?) is Fleitman's for not noting that Biden immediately corrected himself with the actual number at the time: 120 thousand.

Fleitman then claims that Democrats consider Biden mentally unfit, based on overhearing "several conversations." Does Fleitman understand that a few conversations don't represent the views of millions of people? Or is he fictionalizing these conversations in a weak attempt to support his failed argument?

Next, Fleitman absurdly compares Biden to a dying Franklin Roosevelt. He comments that Biden's vice presidential search should look for a "competent chief executive" instead of what he calls "other criteria," specifically "women of color." Fleitman seems unaware that being a woman or a person of color isn't an impediment to being president.

To conclude his column, Fleitman claims he's not giving Donald Trump "a pass" on cognitive competence. But Fleitman actually gives Trump that pass, shrugging his rhetorical shoulders and saying it's "impossible ... to know" about Trump's mental state. Shouldn't a competent writer hold Trump to the same scrutiny that he just tried (unsuccessfully) to apply to Biden?

Of course, Biden isn't perfect. No one is. He's a senior citizen and pretty goofy sometimes. But he shows significant linguistic cognition in overcoming a lifelong stutter, something Fleitman conveniently fails to mention in his attack.

Here are three methods that Fleitman ignores for honestly assessing Biden's mental capacity. First, read Biden's actual platform and watch his full speeches rather than relying on out-of-context snippets. Second, watch all of Trump's speeches and read all of his tweets to contrast him with Biden. The difference is clear.

Third, instead of relying on Trump-supporting concern trolls like Fleitman, let's hear from the actual neurologist who examines Biden. Dr. Neal Kassell has been seeing Biden regularly since operating to repair Biden's brain aneurysms three decades ago. He says Biden's fine.

"I am going to vote for the candidate who I am absolutely certain has a brain that is functioning," Kassell says, "and that narrows it down to exactly one." I'll be voting for Biden as well. That's a no-brainer.

About the Author

John Sheirer (pronounced "shy-er") lives in Northampton, Massachusetts, with his wonderful wife Betsy and happy dog Libby. He has taught writing and communications for nearly three decades at Asnuntuck Community College in Enfield, Connecticut, where he has twice earned Asnuntuck's Educational Excellence and Distinguished Service Award. He serves as editor of *Freshwater Literary Journal* and writes a monthly newspaper column on current events for his hometown newspaper, the *Daily Hampshire Gazette*. His books include memoir, fiction, poetry, essays, political satire, and photography. He has been presented with a Connecticut Green Circle Award to honor his environmental writing, has won the Pinnacle Book Achievement Award, and has been a finalist for the Sante Fe Literary Award and the Next Generation Indie Book Award. His most recent book is *Fever Cabin,* a fictionalized journal of a man isolating himself during the early stages of the current pandemic. (All proceeds from *Fever Cabin* will benefit pandemic-related charities.) Find him at JohnSheirer.com.

9 798683 531928